Can You Hear Me?
The Psychic Animal Communicator

Janine Wilbraham

To Tina
Love from
Janine ☺ x

Local Legend Publishing UK

Janine Wilbraham © Copyright 2011

A Record of this Publication is available
from the British Library

ISBN 978-1-907203-25-1

Edited by Sarah Taylor -Fergusson

Local Legend Publishing 2011
www.local-legend.co.uk

Cover Design by Titanium Design
www.titaniumdesign.co.uk

Cover Photograph by Jacquie Blake

For more information about Janine and her work go to:
www.horsecommunicator-reikihealer.co.uk

Dedication

I dedicate this book to the memory of all the horses that have lost their lives whist being transported long-distance for slaughter.

May they, at last, find peace.

Acknowledgements

I would like to thank so many people it would take far too many pages, but thanks must go to my grandmother Alice, my mother Lily, and Tony my father, who have helped me over the years and gave me the confidence to write this book. My heartfelt thanks go, too, to the wonderful animals in my life. Especially the horses – Angel, Amber, Cloud, Goliathe, Chance, Tiggy, Susy and Tess... The list is endless.

Thanks also to the people in the book who allowed me to speak to their animals and, of course, their wonderful animals.

Thank you to Jayshea and Sandi and my boys, and David, without whom my house would still be unliveable!

And Sarah Taylor-Fergusson, for her editing work and making this book possible.

There are lots I have missed out, and you will know who you are, I thank you all for coming into my life and helping me on this wonderful path.

Contents

Introduction

This is a totally truthful account of my communications with horses and other animals over the years. It starts with when I was a little girl and did not have a name for what I was doing, and when the practice was not generally accepted, and goes up to and includes my current work with horses and other animals as a professional psychic, which I have been involved with for the last twenty-five years.

I live in beautiful rural Mid-Wales, along with my horses, cats, dogs, peacocks and pet sheep. As well as my work as a horse and animal communicator, I practise as a qualified Reiki healer master teacher and riding instructor and appear on the Sky TV psychic channel as a clairvoyant. I am also a community councillor and coordinator for my local Friends of the Earth group. I have studied law and passed a HNC in Scottish law whilst living in Scotland. I have moved home ten times from England to Wales to Scotland and back to Wales. Meeting various interesting people and animals along the way has woven and added into the tapestry of my life.

For more information about Janine and her work visit her website at:
www.horsecommunicator-reikihealer.co.uk

1

Miss Doolittle and the Gypsies

I was born an only child – or so I thought, but that is another story – in the West Midlands. Due to the break-up of my parents' marriage, my grandmother, my mother's mother, Alice Smith, who I called Nan, raised me.

We lived in a semi-detached house in a suburb of Birmingham with her children, my aunts. Nan was a strict Methodist and we attended chapel every Sunday. I also went to Sunday school which I liked at first. My grandfather had passed into spirit before I was born.

However, as a small child, it was not church which had captured my imagination, but animals. Always, animals. I was drawn to them, as if to a magnet, and drove everyone mad wanting first a horse, then a dog, a cat, in fact everything and anything I might be allowed. But, sadly, due to the fact that my grandmother was still working, I wasn't allowed any kind of a pet.

And so I found other people's animals to befriend, and where we lived that meant the gypsies . . . I used to walk up to their horses on the common land and talk to them, or sit for ages just watching them. The horses used to talk back to me. It is hard to explain how they talked to me when it is something I have become completely used to, but what they said to me came in the form of feelings, pictures and words. They used to tell me how they felt about things – sometimes this could be sad or painful. Holding out my hands to the horses, I used to feel my skin heat up, and the horses would sleep, soothed by my touch. Slowly, the gypsies – not the most accepting of people due to others' frequent mistrust of and fear of bad luck from them – got used to this strange child in their midst, and came to accept me. I absolutely hated it when they moved on and waited, every year, for their return.

It did not end with just the gypsies' horses. Everything I could lay my hands on got the 'Janine' treatment. I would stroke or just hold out my hands and ask God to help me heal the animals.

8

Some creatures that were ill got better; others just wanted to be in my company. Quickly, I was given the nickname Miss Doolittle. Neighbours' cats and dogs were fussed over, and people were amazed how animals came up to me.

When I was seven, Nan seemed to accept that I was different to most other children, and that I talked of things which came to happen, not long afterwards. One shocking occasion concerned Nan's elderly next-door neighbour, who wasn't fond of me for playing Nan's piano when she was out. She lived next door and hated my attempts of banging and crashing on it – something I wasn't allowed to do. This time I was sitting on the wall outside our house waiting for Nan to get home from her morning's work as a cleaner. I was meant to be with another lady who lived down the road, but she wasn't a good time-keeper and regularly sent me home before the allotted time. I had been on the piano and had then gone to sit on our wall and wait. The neighbour came out and gave me a mouthful, telling me in no uncertain terms what she would tell my grandmother, and that then I would be in trouble. Well, as I stared at her all I could see was a white face which looked like an old doll and before I could think them back in, out of my mouth came the words, 'It doesn't matter as you will be dead by Saturday.'

My grandmother arrived before the neighbour had finished telling me what she thought of me. Consequently, I wasn't allowed out to play with my friends. But, two days later, there was a commotion next door which woke me up. In the morning there was an uncomfortable silence around the breakfast table. My aunts would not look at me and Nan seemed agitated. Once everyone else had left the house, she asked me about my run-in with the neighbour and why I had said what I had said to her. When I explained, she looked worried and told me to tell no one. The problem was the lady who had died had told her daughter what I'd said. So I was no longer allowed to play with the children next door. People on the estate looked at me oddly and seemed even a little fearful of me and I could not understand why.

Months later, I was out with my father. He was visiting a friend of his and so I was playing with the children in the street. There was an older boy there who I knew as David who was in a wheelchair. He wore a cap and always had a smile for everyone. He used to turn the skipping rope for us. This time, it was my turn to jump and as I did, I looked at David. I was seeing the same thing again – his face was white and frozen in a grimace, like the old lady's had been. I remember screaming and running in to fetch my dad, saying that David was dead. My father and his friend rushed out immediately to find David still turning the rope. You can imagine the trouble I was in. Everyone said what a horrid child I was, and I was taken home there and then and sent to bed early, with the threat of boarding school ringing in my ears – as I didn't know what that was, I was filled with fear.

Now, I only ever saw my father on a Friday and a Sunday, so it was very unusual to have him turn up on a Monday. Listening at the door, I heard him telling my grandmother that David had died the night before, my dad had heard the news at work, so he had come straight round. After he left, my Nan called me in and asked me again to recount what I'd seen. When I'd finished, we sat way past my bedtime talking.

Nan told me that I had a gift that my great-granny had had, but people would be afraid of it, so I must be careful what I said in future. She was frightened for me that people would brand me as someone who was capable of making things happen, as back then people were immediately suspicious. Nan said, 'It's not the done thing to tell people, and people will think you're odd.'

After that, I was more careful with what I said. From then on, my grandmother would sit with me on her lap, and we would read the open coal fire together, making caverns in the coal and making up stories that we saw coming to life in the glow of the flames. Of course, I now realize she was teaching me, although she never once mentioned the word psychic. Nan was what is known as a 'knower', who used to know instinctively if people were good or bad and what was going to happen. Part of her family came from Ireland and this talent came down both sides of the family, and also from my grandfather's side; his mother was Irish and also had the 'sight'.

The summer when I was ten, before I was sent away to boarding school, was a memorable one. The gypsies had returned to their camp near us and although almost everyone else was unhappy about their arrival, I was delighted. I was there the very next day, excited as can be. I hung about at the back of the camp, watching, and eventually the horses and ponies grew curious and came closer. The gypsies had given up telling me to go, and this time one old gypsy man approached me. I had been warned not to go into the caravans in case I was stolen by them. The idea of being stolen by the gypsies thrilled me, as I couldn't think of anything better than spending all my time with their horses. But, try as I might, I was never stolen, so I can only assume that they didn't want me!

The elderly man asked me why I watched the horses and if I could ride. I had to admit that, no, I had sat on the 'rag man's' horse but could not ride one. It seemed important to tell the truth, so I told him that I talked to them – and that they talked back to me. Amazingly, he didn't burst out laughing. Even more amazingly, he sat down beside me and, chewing on a blade of grass, he asked me what they said to me. But first, I had a question for him. I wanted to know if gypsies stole children. He looked shocked then laughed and said no, they had too many of their own to feed! When I had swallowed back my disappointment, I started telling him what his horse had said to me.

The horse was a black and white gelding, what they call a gypsy cob. He told me that he had a pain in his foot and that it was hot. I asked him how he had got the pain and he told me the dog had bitten him and it hurt. All this was said without words passing out loud. I told the gypsy what he told me. The man looked at me oddly and asked which one. I pointed to it. He went over and picking up his foot, checked it out and felt around his heel and looked totally shocked when he saw blood on his fingers. I told him I could heal horses, and they liked it. He asked me to show him. Holding my hands out and facing the horse I felt heat surge through and the horse's breathing slowed, his head drooped and he promptly fell asleep. I knew without a doubt that this man trusted me. Finally here was someone who believed me, and I was invited inside his family caravan for some stew.

I listened to the gypsies talk and could not understand a word. They were speaking in their own language, Romany. As they talked, they kept looking at me, and the man's wife laughed – she obviously didn't believe him – but he seemed to be insisting to her. In the end, she invited me back, and so I spent every day of the summer holidays there, turning up in the mornings after breakfast, going home for lunch, and then returning in the afternoons. My grandmother thought I was playing out on my bike with my friend, and I didn't dare tell her where I was. I got away with it for weeks, but then one day the gypsies came round to our house, selling their wooden dolly pegs, and I was recognized as the horse girl. I had some explaining to do. All too soon, the summer ended and then it was September and I was sent away to boarding school.

Even though I was away at school, there was always the summer holidays, when I would spend as much time with the gypsies as I could. No one on the estate played with me any more; not only was I an 'odd child' but I went to a 'posh school'. One summer when I arrived back home for the holidays, I rushed to get my bike and cycle out to see if the gypsies had arrived, only to find the plot of land that had been their camp turned into a building site. I never saw them again.

Years later, I was to meet up once more with gypsies, or travellers as they were called in Scotland, and fall for a man who was a traveller, and live with him for twelve years of my life.

2
School and Training:
Cannock Chase to Cheshire

The years I was away at boarding school passed in a blur. The school had the rather wonderful name of Shooting Butts, and it was in Cannock Chase, Staffordshire. It was actually a mixed boarding school, which was unusual then, but has long since closed down. I was there from age ten to fifteen and was always in trouble.

I found conforming to certain rules difficult. Even mealtimes were not much fun. Cheese triangles were sneaked out in my pocket for a game in the dormitory. I would throw them, my friend Joy would try to grab them and I would sling them at the ceiling, where they stuck. It was when I was using a book to attempt to knock the cheese triangle down, making even more of a mess than before, when the teacher walked in. After the biggest telling-off, we were made to scrub the whole dorm, and clean everyone's shoes and pumps – no mean feat.

The punishment for the boys at school was the slipper. I got it once, shortly before it was stopped for girls – and then for boys too. Being slippered in front of the whole school was an awful experience, but I can't say it made me behave any better. I would just retaliate more. Walking across the lawn – which divided the boys from the girls – was forbidden, although that didn't stop me. I picked up a detention for that. New teachers would ask for me, Katharine and Joy to stand up and tell them who was who, as they had been warned we were disruptive. Now I feel sorry for the teachers who had to control me. When I could, I would sneak off across the backs to sit in peace and quiet or to eat the berries off the elder trees. Mostly, though, the teachers were nice, but I hated being there. One teacher in my second year – Miss Uppertis (she was called some rude names by the boys) – took to me. She had a lovely puppy that I played with. I was sad when she was moved on to teach another year as she was excellent.

13

I made friends with a cow in a field next to the school playing fields. She would put her head in my hands and speak to me. She told me that she hated losing her babies and she had a lot of them and never knew where they went, I told her about not seeing my mother and that she would see them again, I of course then did not realize that they had gone for meat but I hope it gave her some peace of mind. My school friends thought I was nuts – until of course I told them things about their families they couldn't know.

One girl asked me to see her future, and I kept getting her leaving the school and going away. This didn't make any sense to us. But, after the summer holidays she returned in floods of tears – her family were emigrating to Australia and she was leaving. After this, the girls weren't sure if I had made it happen or if I had simply seen it. It was of course the latter, and I couldn't change what I saw. But I did notice a sort of wary acceptance of me and people wanting to be friends rather than fall out with me.

Our second year was spent in another part of the school which was called Pipewood. This was still in Cannock Chase but about five miles away. We moved back into the main building for our third year and beyond. Anyway, it was while I was at Pipewood that I very nearly died.

We were out on a walk when I took a shortcut – and started to sink into quicksand. I couldn't feel any ground under me, but I could feel the mud pulling me down. Panicking, I shouted for help. Luckily some girls came running and a tall, big-framed girl lay on top of the mud while her friend held her feet and another went for help. By now I was up to my waist in it. She told me to stay still, but even so, I was soon in up to my shoulders in muddy water and was convinced I was going to die. While we waited for the firemen she held onto me, all the time talking to me. By the time the firemen arrived, everyone around me was silent, I was worn out and the water was starting to enter my mouth. But they managed to pull me free, and I have never forgotten Veronica, who saved my life. After that, the area was closed off and warning signs put up.

I suppose my gift should have warned me about this, and in a way it did; I knew as I crossed the muddy ground that I had to turn back, but I didn't listen to myself and chose to ignore the warning.

What happened was a harsh lesson and I would heed it well in future.

I left school at fifteen with no qualifications whatsoever as I sat through every exam writing simply 'don't know' on the paper. All I wanted to do was to leave school and work with horses and it couldn't come quickly enough. In later years, however, I went on to do evening classes in English, Latin, biology and law, which is my favourite subject. I have also completed a university degree and a HNC qualification and worked as an adviser for the Citizens Advice Scotland.

I went on to a large equestrian training centre to learn how to ride properly. My parents had found me a place in Wilmslow, Cheshire, which took on working pupils. It was my dream, although the work was hard and I didn't realize how much I didn't know about horses until then. The work with the horses was long but what I loved – but I couldn't take the theory and the constant criticism. Nothing was right, and if a horse had a speck of dirt on him you were sent back to wash him until he was clean. Since I was usually given a grey horse the 'blue bag' was used often, and the horse didn't like it much either.

But what I found really difficult was that the horses spoke to me – often telling me they were unhappy, despite the fact that they were looked after very well. On one occasion I told an instructor that the horse I was riding had a hurt back and didn't want to be ridden. I was so ridiculed that I never said anything ever again, but at night I would slip out and heal the horses. One horse there called Gay Sorrow was a stunning chestnut mare, and I had some pony club exams to do my C and B, I was so nervous but she really got me through it and I passed first time.

Although my training was meant to be for three years, I could only stick two. I found it too difficult to cope with the increasingly loud voices of the horses complaining that they didn't like the regime and didn't want to be ridden. Not every one of them though was unhappy, however I felt helpless. Even today I still think of them and wonder if I could have changed things for them. This was the first time I felt as if I'd let horses down.

3

Stables, Rescue and Riding School Horses

After leaving the equestrian training centre in Cheshire, I moved nearer home, staying with my mother and stepfather. I was able to complete my training at a nearby stables, where I found work. Here there were riding horses for the school, and liveries, horses that were stabled and in part looked after for their owners. Also, rescue horses were taken in.

It quickly became chaos as the horses realized I could hear them, and they tried to speak to me. Whenever I went into the field, they all followed me. I found it draining to try and make promises which I might not be able to keep. And the horses showed me things which were so upsetting I found it hard to cope at times. A lot of the horses were rescues or were purchased from sales; the owner had a soft spot for any ill looking or depressed animals, and she was involved in horse welfare so we had all sorts. These poor animals would tell me about the things that had happened to them. One horse had been a show jumper and his legs were tender and covered with bumps. He told me that to make him jump higher the pole had been fixed (this is called rapping their legs). When he could no longer win any prizes he had been left in a field, with little food, and was often cold. Others told me of riders that had mistreated them and people so heavy on their backs that they were still in pain from back problems.

Once the horses were OK they were used in the riding school but never overworked and they seemed to enjoy their new life. The ones that were not keen on different riders would, if the right person wanted them, be sold to vetted new owners.

All of us working at the stables had our own yards to look after as well as the riding school horses. One day on arriving at my yard I experienced this feeling of doom and total panic. I couldn't shake it off. When we went to fetch the horses in from the field the feeling intensified and the noise in my head grew louder; it felt like I was drowning. I had to tell the other girl who was there working

16

with me, and she seemed to believe me. We got the horses in and then went to fetch the others – but one was missing, a horse called Ureock. We searched everywhere. I asked him where he was and he showed me water. We couldn't think where it was, but then we remembered the canal.

We ran there so fast I could hardly breathe, and there poor Ureock was; he had fallen in. The gates were closed and the section he was in had filled up with water. I remember jumping in and trying my best to hold up his head, to save him from drowning. People appeared and the gates were opened to let the water out. The horse was still struggling and I had to get out, although I didn't like leaving him. But by this time the fire brigade had arrived, and they managed, with the help of a vet, to calm him and lift him out. Very sadly, though, we were too late to save his legs, which were broken, and he had to be put down. I couldn't get him and the feeling that I had let him down, out of my mind.

After this incident I vowed that never again would I not act on my instinct, even though it would get me into trouble over the years. But I don't regret anything. I knew also that many people thought that I was making it all up, that I couldn't talk to animals; or they were wary, because even though they didn't really believe me, they were worried about what their pets might be saying.

In the yard I ran was a lovely horse called Donella. She was a grey, very pretty Arab type. She was also incredibly nervous, which made her difficult to work with. The first time I spoke to her she looked at me with the biggest eyes. I practised asking her to do things for me, like walk to the manger or to come to me. Slowly she learnt to trust me. She became confident – as long as I wasn't sitting on her back. Being an animal communicator doesn't make you a good rider; I think it can have the opposite effect as you hear all your horse's thoughts and pick up on their fears, which can make you nervous and jittery in return. The horse picks up on your mood and, suddenly, you are into real problems. You could say I had some very eventful rides. In those days I was definitely a better groom than I was a rider.

My boss bought some horses from a sale, one of which was a pretty chestnut mare called Cameo. As soon as I saw her I wanted this little mare, who was only 14.2 hh. We hit it off. When I backed her she was a major problem. It turned out that she had been backed before but she was like a horse at a rodeo. How I managed to stay on her, I will never know, but slowly we became used to each other. Soon, she would do anything for me, and me for her, and for many years she was my companion. Once I left the stables I kept Cameo there, and when I moved then to a stud yard in Derbyshire, Cameo came with me.

Folly was a 13.2 hh pony that was ridden in the riding school. I loved him dearly and every morning when I got off the bus he would be waiting for me, and I would climb on his back and ride down the field to the stables, where he would be given a treat. When Folly was sold I was devastated. At 13.2 hh he was really too small for me to ride for very long, and I couldn't in any case afford to buy him, but neither of these things influenced how I felt about him. The day that he was taken away was horrible; he shouted, I cried, and I never saw him again. Over the years I often wondered if he was OK and so I tried tuning in to him to see if I could get any messages. Sometimes images did come into my mind and he did seem to be telling me that he was all right, but I never was sure if this was how it was or if I was just trying to make myself feel better.

It wasn't just horses at the stables that I talked to. Topaz the stable cat used to get through to me after I had left to try and tell me things. But while I was still there, I became known for being good with both horses and dogs. They would do most things for me and horses that were classed as bad would behave in my company. The other liveries would ask for help and I found it hard not to give it. So weekends were spent back working at the stables and only giving lessons to people on their own horses. I found it handy being a horse communicator as I would 'hear' when the horses were starting to be naughty or were about to start playing up and could stop things before they got out of hand.

4

Wales to Scotland and Back to Wales Again

After finishing at the stables, I went for a job in Derbyshire. I landed the job, met a man and got married, all within six weeks! At the same time I started doing readings for people, helped with healing both at the local church and for people who came to me at home. I also started to read animals for people who were receptive to the idea of it. However, it wasn't until I hit my twenties that I decided to do this full-time – as well as studying law.

I was perfecting my art and learning to meditate. For anyone wanting to dip into the psychic world, I suggest that meditation is the way forward. I cover this in detail in a later chapter. I was choosing my path, and this was one which brought horses, dogs and cats to me. Many of these animals were misunderstood, which was so sad, but there were others which had owners who were doing their very best to help their pets find peace of mind. I took on a lot of rescued animals and frequently did communications for little money or for free.

My personal life wasn't an easy one, though, which may seem strange since I was helping animals and their owners whenever I could. For myself, I seemed to choose the wrong path, repeatedly. I was married twice, first to Eddie, then to Andy – and had four beautiful children – and then I met the love of my life. But this was a relationship which could be destructive and sometimes violent. And I ended up moving around a lot because of this.

Although I had moved to Scotland because I wanted somewhere suitable for my horses, I was, in fact, hoping to move deeper into Wales. I felt an affinity for this part of the world, even though I had been born in the Midlands. At this time no property in the right price range was available, and so I put my wishes to one side and started looking for somewhere in Scotland instead. While reading a property paper, I came across a croft in the far north of

Janine Wilbraham

Scotland, near John O'Groats, Caithness. It came with seventeen acres, had sea views and was cheap. The ten-hour journey hadn't managed to put me off, so I made an offer on the croft – only then realizing that, due to Scottish property laws, I was bound to buy it! There was a mad panic as I tried to sell my other house and move.

Luckily, my soon to be ex-husband and a friend helped me move. Over the weekend, doing round-the-clock trips, we moved horses, peacocks, geese, dogs and two of my children. The other two children wanted to stay in Wales, one to join the army, the other to live with his stepfather.

Caithness was an eye-opener – literally. The wind was like nothing else I have known. At times it blew so hard you couldn't hear the television. The power was often down in the winter too. I found it hard to understand the local accent at first; not knowing anyone was difficult and I was homesick for Wales. While the children were at school I would walk for miles along the shoreline. I came to love the solitude and how the seals would come close to see the dogs. Only the gulls in the air above screamed their anger at my intrusion. But I loved the place and got on well with the villagers. When my other two sons Klint and Kane moved up to stay with me, before finding a cottage of their own which was only a few miles away, I felt at home.

Those first years in Caithness were a magical time. My youngest son, Ashley, only nine years old at the time, used to come with me to a beauty spot called Samuel's Geo, south of Freswick Bay, where broad-topped stacks of horizontal sandstone had become isolated from the main part of the cliffs. We would sit for ages looking out to sea, and Ashley would sit so still, playing his recorder, watching in amazement as the seals drew nearer and nearer, their heads popping up to glimpse us and listen to the simple music. I did try and communicate with the seals, and did receive some information back, but mainly they gave me feeling, and to this day it is still difficult to put into words how they communicated with me.

If we found birds that had been injured we took them in to heal them. Once my daughter, Jayshea, came home with an injured swan; it had flown into the power line and damaged its wing. It was shaken up after its fall. How my daughter caught it and carried it

20

home I have no idea, but a sheet was mentioned! We nursed the bird back to health and then took it to a local man who kept all manner of feathered friends and was a lot more capable than us of looking after it.

I had been living in Caithness for nearly three years when I met my next partner, Hugh. As soon as I saw him I was smitten. He was dark-haired, dark-eyed, muscular and of traveller descent. His grandfather had lived in a cave, and his mother had travelled the roads, living in a tent. He had been brought up in a house, as by then his mother had settled, but they were still called travellers. He reminded me of the gypsies I had known, and spent so much time with, as a child. We lived together for twelve years. I can't say those years were the happiest of my life as a lot happened, and there was jealousy and anger as well as passion, but, I will never forget him, and when I left Scotland I feel I left a little piece of my heart behind in Caithness.

Sixteen years after I left the Marches of the English–Welsh border, I came back home to live in Wales. My children – mostly grown up by now – moved down to settle in Wales and to be with me. First, Ashley, then my daughter, Jayshea, and finally my twin sons, Klint and Kane, and Klint's girlfriend and two children. Not one to do things by half, I bought a semi-derelict house that was to take me four years to do up with lots of help from my family. But I knew that once I had finished working on it, I would be over my ex-lover.

Twelve years of living in an emotional state had taken their toll on my health and I needed to put the past behind me and recover my energies. Self-healing helped, as did my horses Angel and Amber and my dogs, Susie a bearded collie, Fiag my Scottish deer hound, Tess, a little rescue Jack Russell cross Lakeland terrier, also old Mr Duck and my rescued pigeon. We were an odd group but we got on well together. Work on the house helped occupy my thoughts, and I threw myself into working as a psychic on TV using a webcam. And as I started to become known in Mid-Wales, the work started to flood in, and I gave lots of private readings and horse communications. I would work from six in the morning until late, sometimes not finishing until I fell into bed at night. But mostly it was Angel and Amber who got me through.

Janine Wilbraham

Angel and Amber

5

How I Communicate with and Heal Horses

The very first thing that I do when I meet a new horse is to stand back and wait to be invited into their presence. This is important, as we all have a tendency to barge in on animals, not giving them the respect they deserve. Think about how you feel when someone approaches you and stands too close; it makes you uncomfortable. Well, horses are the same; they appreciate politeness, and you will get far by being polite with them.

Even when all I have is a photograph of a horse – perhaps because the owner hasn't been able to get the horse to travel to see me – I still do this as the preliminary to the communication, making the connection wait. Only when the horse is ready do I ask if it is OK for me to speak to them. I get some varying results to this – frequently amazement, followed by surprise – but then they usually don't mind at all.

Horses are very spiritual animals and their energy is powerful. They can be badly misunderstood. And what people don't realize is that horses read them the minute they meet. They can read our aura (the aura is an energy field that surrounds every living thing), and tell what sort of a mood we are in, be it angry, nervous, happy, and know if you are an OK sort of person. Some horses can even read our minds – as many owners will testify when they are taking their horse to a show.

If the horse is in a stable, I stand outside the door and read their aura. I will then send them love, from my heart. Since I love animals this is very easy for me to do. Usually, the horse will then look at me or come over. I offer my hand with my palm down to them, never forcing my hand into their space. And I don't straight away scratch their withers or neck as I haven't had permission to. Think how you might feel if a stranger started playing with your hair or your neck! Then I regulate my breathing, so the horse who might be a bit fearful can tune into it and feel calm. Only then do I enter their stable.

So once the horse – or dog or cat – has granted me permission to begin, I start to speak and communicate with them. I will send them love, and they always like receiving it. Next, I ask general questions and ask them what they would like to tell me. The information I get back doesn't always come in the form of words, it can also be pictures, symbols, colours or feelings. Usually the animal's owner has some questions they want answered, so I ask those, and relay back the replies. Sometimes an animal doesn't want to answer a particular question. If this happens I will leave it, and return to it later, asking it in a different way. Animals don't talk like we do, in long conversations; they use stilted type sentences, although a few can be good talkers.

And for me, it doesn't really matter whether I have the horse or animal there in front of me or just a picture of them; as a natural-born clairvoyant I find this comes easily.

Once I have finished communicating with the animal, I thank them for allowing me to speak to them, and I gently stroke them. I never slap or clap a horse; I wouldn't like it so why should they? Usually, if they have had a healing they will be feeling a bit sleepy, and will go and have a drink.

I like to give the owners some verification, and this can be most unusual at times. I never judge the owners as it isn't my place to do so and everyone has their own way of looking after their animals. But I do have to be very careful of what I tell them since sometimes the owner and their animal don't get on and once I have left they still need to relate to each other. Horses are, though, very forgiving animals and only rarely dislike their owners. Sometimes it is interesting to ask myself whose decision it was first – the horse or the owner – to instigate change.

Many people ask for readings or communications because they are thinking of selling their horse and would like clarification, and to check that the horse is OK with their plan. Often they have encountered problem after problem with the animal and no longer feel they are capable of helping it. They come hoping that I will be able to point the way forward. The horse may tell me that they need another home, but this isn't always the case, and sometimes after a chat with the horse their behaviour will change. In those instances I work on advising the owner and keep in touch with them via email or phone to see how the relationship is progressing. Sometimes I will be called back to give more healing to the horse and their rider. When an owner isn't interested in selling their horse, they might just want to know more about their horse's past, and if any problems have developed, what has caused it.

When a horse gives me colours it can be connected to the horse's chakras, and so if a particular colour is given I will put my hand on the area that it is representing. For example, if a red colour is given, the animal might be having problems in their base or root chakra, in a horse, this is situated at the top of the tail. Usually horses with problems in their root chakra are quite fearful.

During the communication, I can give healing to the area to balance it. In brief, the seven main chakras of the body are: the base – red; the sacral – orange; the solar plexus – yellow; the heart – green; the throat – blue; the third eye – indigo; the crown – violet.

If a horse or an animal has pain, they will show it to me in my body, and it can be quite sharp. Sometimes the feelings can be very painful and it isn't unusual to find me with tears coursing down my face – not a pretty sight as I wear black eye make-up! But this stage is important as this is the horse's feelings, and once I have experienced it, the pain can start to leave them. Of course, it can upset me too as I am so fond of horses. When this happens I have to try and push it out of my mind. The healing I can offer works brilliantly alongside the conventional treatment given by a vet; in fact, it is often best to start by asking your vet's advice first.

Which is probably a good place to mention something which does concern me: some animal communicators claim that an animal can diagnose a problem or read his blood results. Now, in all my years of working with animals, I have never come across one who is a doctor or can read! So please be aware that, unfortunately, there are some people out there who are not genuine animal communicators – although it is possible that if they are clairvoyant, they may be picking up the information themselves rather than via the animal. In this respect, horses and other animals are no different to people: we can say when we have feelings of pain, but we can't know for sure what is causing them without a doctor's help. With animals, only a vet can make that diagnosis; it is not up to the layman, or me, to guess.

I have found that animals love healing, and that horses in particular appreciate it. Quite often even horses that have been badly treated by people will return the favour and send healing back to me, which is very nice. Although it doesn't work in the same way as the healing that I send, as it doesn't make me sleepy, it does give me a warm glow and a feeling of peace.

I understand that many people can't fathom how long-distance healing can be of any help whatsoever. The idea that you can send healing to an animal or a person who is somewhere else rather than right in front of you is a strange concept for some. But I can assure you that it does work. As communication is done via energy, it doesn't really matter if it is a picture of the animal or if the animal is there in front of me; the energy is the same, and as a natural-born clairvoyant, I suppose I find this a lot easier than most other people do.

As just one example, I sent healing to a lady's horse in America, not telling her what time I was doing it, and before I had chance to tell her, she reported back that it had worked. She was amazed, and her relationship with her horse started to improve from that moment. Before contacting me, she had been on the verge of giving up riding altogether, but now they go off on trail rides of two or three days at a time, enjoying each other's company, which is something she could only have dreamed about previously. The communication helped the owner understand the horse better, and it also helped the horse relate to its owner.

I never force healing on an animal without its permission, though. Perhaps in the last twenty years there has only been one horse that has refused it, and that animal was so badly emotionally damaged I felt that he probably couldn't have coped with the healing. I think he may have felt he was unable to let his guard down even for that and was happier being switched off from any emotion, even positive ones. He had been rescued, but had undergone some terribly traumatic things which are too upsetting to describe in this book. The positive thing which I try to remember is that for the last six months of his life he was cared for properly and was finally able to find peace and quiet. And when he died, he wasn't alone.

Throughout my life, I have met many people and horses, and it isn't just the horses owned by the wrong sorts of people on low incomes who can be mistreated and misunderstood. Among those who compete, there are of course many who love their horses dearly. But there are also those who want to compete at any cost.

They have all the gear, the best food and the tidiest yards, but their horses are not happy. They are not living like horses should, going out, interacting with other horses, having fun, getting messy. They don't really interact with other horses in case they get kicked, and it is these horses that my heart goes out to. For once they are no longer useful to their owners, they end up in sales. While some go on to caring homes, others find that the five-star lifestyle they are accustomed to is no longer theirs and it can take them a long time to adjust. I have seen ex-race horses who suddenly find themselves, literally, out in the cold, and some of them do prefer the pampered life.

While I read for a large number of horses in the UK and abroad, including high-profile people and celebrities, to me all people I read for are the same and receive no different treatment. It doesn't faze me when someone famous contacts me, and I would never brag about it or mention their name. Whoever they are, they have trusted me to help them, and so I respect their confidentiality.

The feedback I get from clients is brilliant, as in almost all the cases there is a vast improvement. And both clients and animals go on to enjoy their lives. I do warn people, though, that it can change your life. One lovely lady I went to see in North Wales changed her life around and has now become more spiritual and a healer. If nothing else, it shows to people that there is a link there that we can all tap into.

6
Animals in Spirit

As well as communicating with the living, I also speak a lot to animals in spirit, and this offers some comfort to owners who are feeling their loss. It is really nice to be able to let the owner know that they are OK and that they are near. And for some reason, I find that animals stay closer than humans do once they have passed over. It is as if they want to make absolutely sure that the owner is able to cope before they can leave them. And even then they come back to check up on us.

An old horse of mine was a lovely Clydesdale mare called Cloud. Cloud was thirty-three years old, which is old for a horse, but I'd had her for just six years. When I got her she was very ill, in a poor condition, and after her years with me it reached the point where no amount of healing could prolong her life any longer. Cloud told me it was time for her to move on, but I found it impossible to let her go. I wouldn't trust my judgement, or felt too emotional to reach a decision. It was just too hard. Finally it was the vet who made the decision for me.

Afterwards, I knew I had to let the other horses know that Cloud had passed over. I always let them see a horse once it is dead so that they know for sure what has happened, rather than thinking the horse has been taken away to be sold or to a new home. My other three horses at the time, Angel, Billy and Chance, ran up the field to find Cloud. I knew that Angel had seen two others leave this world but Chance had not. I was worried about his reaction. He had known Cloud since he had been with me aged two.

When they found Cloud, Angel and Billy stood back, snorting, but Chance tried to get her to get up. It was distressing to watch him paw and nip at her and roar. Eventually, Chance came away but throughout the day he would go and check up on her and would stand guard over her.

When the man came to bury Cloud, we put Chance in his stable. But day after day he would go and stand by her grave. It was

Cloud

about a week later, around nine o'clock in the evening, and I was out grooming the horses. The first I knew was that Chance, in his stable, which was next to Cloud's old one, was neighing and snorting like mad. I looked out to see what was wrong and there she was: Cloud was stood at the door. The sight of her brought a huge lump to my throat and tears were pouring down my face as she asked me to let her inside.

I communicated with her, explaining that she no longer needed doors to be open, she could go anywhere she wanted. Since that evening, Cloud has returned at least three times. I wondered if she was coming to calm Chance down. I asked him and he said he needed her close and had asked for her to come back. It was the first time I had heard a horse do that before, but it was nice to know they could.

It is not just horses who have died who have returned to my house to visit. Suzie was a bearded collie dog of mine who had suffered from cancer. She had a leg removed because of her illness, but made a good recovery. When I made the move to Mid-Wales, she travelled down with me from Scotland, helping me settle into the new house.

Suzie was a very faithful dog and when she passed over aged twelve I was devastated to lose my loyal companion. The other dogs also missed her. However, on many occasions, visitors who have come to my house have asked after the three-legged dog seen running through the trees, and who did it belong to? It is nice to know she is still around me and the other animals. And that your animals do stay close and come back to visit from time to time.

Suzie

Another dog was Spangle. His owner had passed over and Spangle had spent time in kennels, where he hadn't settled well, before he was rehomed with a couple with no children. The couple had recently lost their spaniel and it was felt that they would be an ideal match.

Spangle, though, appeared to have some issues, and so the couple brought him to see me. One of his habits was that of staring for a long time into the corner of the room; another was barking excitedly when there was no one else around. When I first met Spangle, he was indeed full of beans and excited at seeing my peacocks and ducks. I started to communicate with him.

He said he quite liked his new family and that they were kind to him. But he then told me he couldn't stay as he was about to leave and go with his old owner to a new place to live. I found this very odd. I asked him if he knew that his old owner had gone to spirit, but Spangle didn't seem to understand and told me that he saw his old owner every day. Eventually, it dawned on me: the dog was seeing spirit. In addition to this, to make things more complicated still, his old owner was very attached to him, while his new owners were over the moon as Spangle was helping them to get over the loss of their previous dog.

I had a feeling that Spangle would go to spirit sooner than was expected. I had to break the news to his new owners that his old owner who had passed on was visiting the dog. To my relief, they had already sensed something was up and had even seen something, but hadn't believed it.

I contacted Spangle's original owner through mediumship. She told me that she was upset at losing her dog and was worried about leaving him behind. She wanted him to join her in spirit. I explained to her that Spangle's new owners were going to look after him – and then a thought came to me: I asked her if she would look after their dog that had gone into spirit. I didn't get a reply there and then and she left, so I finished off with giving Spangle some healing. He said he felt very well and thanked me; he was so old-fashioned he made me laugh. Then he and his new owners left.

It must have been about four months later when the couple made another appointment to see me, bringing Spangle. He seemed different. I asked him how things were. He said he was now staying and his old owner was looking after another dog that was ill. She would still come and visit him sometimes and told him she would wait for him when his time came. I felt extremely emotional, for although Spangle's previous owner didn't make contact with me again, she had taken on board what I had said and was now looking after the couple's dog in spirit.

7

Tilly, the Horse who was Misunderstood

Tilly was a lovely fourteen-year-old 15.3 hh thoroughbred mare. She was very fast, very showy, but nervous and edgy with it. She had been purchased for cross-country and riding club activities. Tilly's owner, Madeleine, didn't believe in horse communication – and took pains to tell me this – but she had decided to give it a go since her friend had recommended me. So here she was, along with her horse, to see what would come up.

At first Tilly was exceptionally wary and wouldn't communicate with me at all. To relax her I asked if I could give her some healing. She accepted and gradually was able to settle down. As she relaxed, she started to speak to me.

Tilly told me she had been in about six homes. The second to last home had not been very nice. She was having to compete every week, and was kept in her stable twenty-four hours a day unless she was ridden. Although she was given good food and the best of everything, it wasn't making her happy, as more than anything she wanted to be out in the fields, eating grass. The constant jumping was having a negative effect on her and she was starting to feel pain in her neck and legs, so she tried to stop.

But Sally her owner wasn't happy about this and used the stick more on her to make her jump. Tilly found this difficult and started rearing up in a bid to stop having to go over the jumps. At one competition she totally refused to get out of the box and managed to get away from Sally. She enjoyed it for a short while, snatching at grass in between being chased around.

Within a week, Tilly was at another place, with a man and a woman who had lots of horses that were coming in and out. From what I could gather, this appeared to be a dealer's yard. She did get into a field, though, which was nice, and the woman rode her every day, which she liked too. Madeleine had bought her from this dealer, and moving homes so quickly made Tilly very frightened.

I decided not to relay this information straight away to Madeleine as I wanted to see what Tilly had been doing with Madeleine. All the moving about had left her feeling insecure, and she was wondering where she would end up next. She also felt like a machine and let me know that she was only respected when she was winning. But now she was tired and she didn't want to compete any more.

I knew from experience that this was going to be difficult, so I asked Tilly in my mind if she wanted to stay with her present owner, Madeleine. (I always ask in my mind as it is easy and the animal immediately feels a lot more comfortable knowing that no one else can hear the questions.) Tilly answered that she wouldn't be able to stay with her owner as the woman only wanted to compete.

I never promise horses anything and no one should; we cannot change things for them if they belong to someone else. And in this instance I couldn't afford to buy this mare. If I hadn't had horses of my own already, it might have been possible, but at this time I owned six other horses and I knew that Tilly was very expensive.

I asked Tilly other questions but all she showed me was images of her rearing and not going forward. At least I now knew what the problem was and what Madeleine was experiencing. I was able to tell Madeleine that Tilly was showing me rearing and stopping at jumps. She confirmed that this was the case – and told me that she had purchased her for cross-country and other competitions and that she would have to do this.

This put me in a difficult position. I found it hard not to be cross, however I could also see Madeleine's point of view. When I went on to ask Tilly why she no longer wanted to jump she gave me a picture of her rearing up and going over sideways. She told me it hurt her when she landed, that her bones ached. The energy she gave me was a weary one, and I was picking up painful legs too. From the information she had given me I was able to work out that it wasn't Madeleine on her who was causing the problem.

When I asked Madeleine if the previous owner had mentioned any episodes like this she said she would see if she could find out from people she knew in the area. She was able to tell me, though, that when she had had a lesson recently, Tilly had started to feel a little unsafe and she had been worried she would rear.

My suggestion – that the horse was turned out and given a break for a few weeks – wasn't an option as unfortunately there was a competition coming up and Tilly was expected to compete in it. This was a very awkward situation. The owner had bought the horse to compete on, but the horse didn't want to do it. In this case I couldn't say that the rider was at fault – she wasn't – but it was a case of the horse having had enough. I was worried for Tilly because I sensed that she wasn't going to find the peace she wanted and needed.

All I could do in this situation was to give more healing to Tilly, to her chakras and especially her heart, as I felt she needed it. I asked her to accept her life, although I wasn't comfortable doing this, there was nothing else I could do. Tilly was a lovely mare who wanted just to hack about. She enjoyed being fussed over, but for competing she had gone stale and lost all interest. Madeleine was a kind owner who gave her all the best food and care, but unfortunately horse and owner wanted to go in different directions, and neither were at fault over this.

Three weeks later, Tilly was sent to a dealer's yard, in exchange for a horse more suited to Madeleine's requirements. Madeleine told me she had discovered that Tilly had reared at a competition and that she had started to nap. Napping is a way that horses can tell the owner there is a problem. It can be insecurity or pain related. Usually the horse will not go forward and can become dangerous if they start rearing or bolting. Because of Tilly's napping, Madeleine no longer felt able to carry on with the horse.

Three months passed and I heard that Tilly had been sold again. This time she had become impossible to ride. My heart ached for her. I never heard of her again, so I just hope she is all right.

At times I do come across situations like this one where I am unable to help the horse at all. I give healing to help them cope with their life, but it always gives me a heavy heart to walk away knowing that the issues have not been resolved and there is nothing more I can do. Unfortunately, this is the down side of being an animal communicator.

8
Sale Days

Many horse lovers cannot bring themselves to visit a horse sale –
and they can't believe that I, as a horse communicator, can. While I
find it far from easy, as a natural healer and a Reiki healer/master, I
honestly feel it is my duty to help and heal wherever I can. So from
time to time, I do find myself at the sales.

On this particular occasion I was on my way to a sale over
the border in Leominster near Hereford. This is always a nice sale.
The horses being sold seem to be looked after and there are a lot of
checks done at the sale itself, ensuring that no horses that appear to
be ill are allowed in. There are plenty of stalls, too, selling horse
paraphernalia and also vegetables. This hive of activity is very much
a place to meet up with and chat to regular friends and neighbours.
The 'tack' is sold first – items of saddlery, rugs and riding clothes –
and then at 11 a.m. the horses usually come in. There are a variety of
horses on sale: some come from homes where the owner is going
off to college or who have given up riding, others are old horses that
are no longer wanted since the owner has acquired a younger horse,
and there are ponies from riding schools which are not wanted over
the winter months. All in all, not a bad sale.

I was in the car when the traffic got diverted, and found
myself off the main road on a lane. As I returned to the main road I
felt an overwhelming sense of sadness and tears choking my throat.
Looking back through my rear-view mirror I saw sheep happily
walking along, being herded by farmers to a waiting lorry – all apart
from one. The energy that I was receiving from this one sheep
shocked me. As I looked again in my mirror it seemed to lock eyes
with me and ask for my help.

The feeling this poor sheep gave me was so strong I felt the
tears hot on my cheeks. She was frightened and seemed to know
what fate had in store for her. Sheep are a lot more intelligent than
people give them credit for; they remember people and if hand-
reared will look deep into your face as if reading you. They are

35

nervous animals and run around in groups, but on their own they are totally different.

What could I do? I was stuck in traffic, which was moving slowly, and I had no way of being able to stop the farmer, and even if I did, what on earth would I say? Unfortunately, this is a problem I encounter frequently and living with it is not easy. Sometimes when animals ask for my help I have to say no, which I am not comfortable with. I now try and avoid anywhere where animals are being transported for meat as they do communicate with me. The only thing I can do is send healing and let it help them cope with their situation. It makes me so glad I am a vegetarian.

The Leominster sale was well run and although on that day there was some confusion and one pair of horses desperate not to be parted, which wasn't a nice sight or feeling, most of the horses came across as fine and OK about being there. I didn't stay to the very end, so didn't know how all of them felt about going on to new homes, but it felt a better sale than many I have attended.

The next sale was in my home town, back across the border, in Wales. This sale is an annual fixture and not as nice as the Leominster one. The pens are small and there are a lot of unbroken horses coming off the hills. It is known as a sale where the horses are either lame or not very safe – which is a little unfair as I have purchased two horses from here, both of which were fine. Some of the sellers are very caring and give hay and water to their horses. Unfortunately a lot of them don't, though, which means the animals are standing all day with nothing to eat or drink, which is awful, since horses need to eat eighteen hours a day in small amounts. Plus many of the horses have not been handled before and are terrified of all the noise and the people in the market, who include the local dealers and also the meat man.

On this particular day, when I reached the sale and met up with my friend, we had a good look around and spotted a little Welsh Section A mare who was old and appeared to have problems with her teeth. She was very nervous and quite thin. Her owner came over and started listing all her virtues – but not a bit of it rang true. He could see we were interested, so we made a point of walking round to look at the other horses. When the bidding started we took our seats. It was sad to see the resignation in the horses' eyes, wondering where they were going to end up next.

The little grey mare came through and my friend and I bought her between us for £70. We managed to find someone to take her home, where she settled in well with my friend and her other twenty horses. Later on she had a lovely little foal. Unfortunately, my friend moved away from the area, so I lost track of what happened to the little mare we had named Belle, but I know she would have been OK.

The following year, I went again to my local sale with my daughter Jayshea, and this time I saw a late entry of an old bay mare of eighteen years who was very thin, with a poor conformation, Being a thoroughbred, this was awful to see. She was surrounded by other horses and her ears were flattened to her head; she was attacking anything that came near her, and next to her was a pen of young horses and some lovely ones as well, all two years old. Everyone was muttering about 'the poor old horse'.

The young lad who was with her answered our questions. He assured us that Billy was a quiet horse and he had learned to ride on her. He said that she had to go as she was surplus and he was breaking other horses in. It was the end of October, which is the time of year for people getting rid of their horses, before the winter sets in. Anyway, the lad got on Billy and apart from some evil faces she was OK. But I felt sickened thinking of this eighteen-year-old mare looking so sad and distressed.

I had to weigh up what to do. She was 15.2 hh, so not really big enough for me, and I already had three other horses. My friend and I took our seats and, funnily enough, the only ones we could get together were on a bench at the back, in direct line with Billy, which meant I was able to observe her as the other horses came in. She locked eyes with me across the pens. I felt such a feeling of sadness and despair. She then stood with her head down, apart from when any other horse tried to look at her, when she would lunge from side to side, trying to attack them.

When she came into the ring, you could see that the life had gone out of her. The bidding started and I found myself joining in. Her owners had already let us know they weren't giving her away, and although I think I already knew I was going to buy Billy, I had to discuss it with my daughter and her partner, Byron, first. Luckily they were in agreement. By now there were some horrible comments going round the ring about this old horse, and the bidding was slow; just me and one other bidder. In the end I bought her for £250 – such a small amount it was sad.

Billy was taken back to the stalls and from there it was all go. I had to borrow money as I'd left mine at home. Then my daughter and I had to rush back to fetch the lorry as the sale was nearing its end, leaving Byron paying for her. When we returned, there were only half a dozen horses left, dotted about the venue. She was almost the last to go and had stood all day without food. We put a head collar on Billy and led her to the lorry. She stood while we fitted her with leg protectors and loaded her into the vehicle – or rather she led us, flying up the ramp and once inside, diving for the soiled straw floor, she was so hungry. This was upsetting to see.

We drove Billy home – only a five-mile journey – and put her in the stable. I saw how shocked she was when she set eyes on the hay we put in for her. Billy ate and drank water constantly, then found the salt lick. Poor thing, she looked tired and worn out with her thin neck and sad eyes.

Billy

My other horses came into the stable, but Billy just flew at them in a fury, roaring and threatening them to stay away. They were shocked at her manner. To make her feel safe we ended up putting up boards so that they couldn't look at her. That first night, I checked on her a few times before I went to bed, and she always seemed to be eating, but I did manage to catch her lying down. Normally, horses only lie down if they feel safe, but by now she was so exhausted there was no option.

Billy has been with me for a while now, and she is OK these days, if constantly grumpy and constantly asking if she is going to stay. I can't say she is very friendly, but she is no longer stressed, and sometimes she comes up to me for a fuss. It is difficult to talk to her but at times she tells me some things. She is, though, very guarded and has totally lost her trust in humans. Some things she blanks out, however when you look at her face you can still see the deep groove where a head collar had been left on and became embedded in her face.

A check on Billy's history – the information is only available since her passport came out in 2005 – told me she never stayed anywhere long as she was put through three sales, one of them twice, followed by the one I purchased her from. I tell her that she will never be going to a sale again, that she has a home for life with me and will always have enough to eat.

When people come to do my communication course, the ones who work with her always end up in tears. On the positive side, Billy makes an excellent horse for nervous riders as she is kind and steady when she is being ridden, never putting a foot wrong.

Although the sale at my local town is not my favourite one, I do try to go yearly and send healing and hope to some of the horses like Billy that are there.

9

Psalm the Cat

It's not just horses who I am asked to communicate with. One day I had a phone call from a lady who had lost her black cat. She was very upset and wanted to know if I could look and see where her cat had got to and if she was all right. She was perfectly happy to drive over to visit me, bringing with her a photo of her pet, and pay for the communication. My feeling was, though, that I wouldn't be able to locate the animal, so rather than waste her petrol and money, I asked her to email me a picture of the cat. I would send the cat a message and we would see what happened.

The picture of the cat arrived – a very attractive black Siamese. From this, I had a feeling that Psalm was still in her owner's area. I suggested her owner, Elaine, put up some notices and offered a small reward. Two days later I got the news that she had been spotted and her owner had managed to catch her. She was now wondering if I could speak to her cat. We decided on the following evening.

Psalm arrived in her carrier, not a happy madam at all. She was spitting and meowing, and wanting to be let out. We closed all the doors and let her out. Although she was happy to be fussed over by us and to chat, she didn't give me the information that she belonged to this lady. She let me know that she had a different collar on. She seemed to know this lady, however, and told me that she had two different homes and liked being outside. Then, ever so casually, she sauntered over to the wood burning stove, pulled off her collar, and promptly disappeared up the chimney. Elaine and I were left looking at each other in amazement and shock.

We called up the chimney, we fetched food, we waited – to no avail. I rang my friend who had luckily put a liner in the chimney for me when the wood burner was installed, and he confirmed that she couldn't get out. I then picked up a message from Psalm telling me that she was sat on a ledge, she was perfectly all right and she was going to sleep!

I told her owner this, who informed me that she had been fed before she came over and that when she disappeared it was usually for hours.

So there I was, an animal communicator with a beautiful and expensive Siamese cat up my chimney, possibly never to be seen again. I had awful visions of the local newspaper heading.

Elaine and I decided to go into the kitchen, where we had a much needed cup of tea. We decided on a course of action: Elaine would return home and I would catch Psalm as soon as she came back down. I would ring her owner, who would come back to collect her.

While we were both drinking another cup of tea later on, I received a message from the Siamese saying she was out of the chimney. Like a fool I rushed in, and she shot back up the chimney once more. So, this time, I sat on the floor and asked her to please come back down. Within seconds she was sat in my lap, covered in soot but otherwise perfectly OK.

I then let her know I was going to show her to her owner, and not to be afraid of my dogs, as I would keep her safe. Her owner's face was a picture – and so was Psalm's when she saw my deerhound, German shepherd, terrier and three cats.

We managed to coax her back into her cat basket, and I gave her some healing. Before she fell fast asleep she told me that she liked it here and asked if she could stay with me! I had to tell her it wasn't possible – in any case, I had too many animals already. Psalm let me know that she had lived once at a place like mine. I relayed this to Elaine, who told me she had come from a manor house with land. I felt this was a big compliment: I did have land – but there the similarities ended.

Before Psalm's owner left, she gave me a present of two lovely crystals and a donation to my animal charity. When she got home, she emailed to say that she had given Psalm more Reiki healing and planned to let her out in the morning. She also said that if she wanted to live between two homes, then she could. This, I felt, was a happy resolution to the situation – but it was not to be the end of it.

A further two weeks later, Elaine contacted me to tell me that Psalm the cat had turned up: it turned out that the cat she had brought over to my house wasn't hers after all, which explained why the animal didn't confirm that she belonged to Elaine, and that it was correct, it did have two homes. So now Elaine had her own cat back, and the other black Siamese came in and out now and again to say hello and to have food off her.

Psalm was very thin when she returned to Elaine. She stayed in for a few days, but didn't want to stay in all the time. She has found her own pattern of coming in and out and occasionally vanishing for a few days, always coming back.

Elaine and I had to laugh, at the thought that we could have been prosecuted for cat-stealing. The ending was a happy one, though, and Elaine and I are now friends and keep in touch.

Psalm

10

Jasmine and Kate

A lovely lady called Kate contacted me after seeing my website. She wanted me to communicate with her horse Jasmine and asked if I could come over to see her, also her friend's horse.

I drove across Wales and found the place easily – thank goodness for sat-nav. When I arrived, Kate was waiting for me and Jasmine was in her stable. Kate told me she had purchased the beautifully coloured cob mare recently and some issues had come up.

Jasmine was a very attractive horse but quite opinionated. After her initial shock that I could communicate with her, she opened up to me and gave Kate the information that she needed to start working with her and sorting out her health issues. On that first visit, I also gave her some healing, and this helped with some stiffness she had.

I paid Kate and Jasmine a follow-up visit, and during this Jasmine was quite naughty, not doing as Kate asked, not standing and being a bit nappy (refusing to go forward) at the crossroads near where they lived. So after speaking to Jasmine I decided to try some natural horsemanship with her.

Within minutes she was standing for Kate to mount her, and so off we went down the road. When we reached the crossroads, she refused to turn right, so we worked on moving her forward using reward and release. Very soon she was going up the road, coming back and going up again, all without any force. This was genuine progress. We returned to the stables and Jasmine seemed to have more respect for Kate.

Since then, I have done further readings for Jasmine via email and she has come on amazingly. The health issues have been sorted out and Kate has moved her to a holistic livery yard called the Bitless Bridle Equestrian Centre. Jasmine is in their barefoot and bitless herd environment and is loving it. She looks amazing. The dull, sad look she had is gone. I am so glad that Jasmine ended up with Kate as her owner, because Kate has worked on the mare with consideration and kindness.

Kate and Jasmine are now able to continue with wonderful and sympathetic teaching from the instructor at the equestrian centre, carrying on along the natural path that I started them on. For any ailments which arise, Jasmine is receiving natural and manual medicine from an equine therapist who the centre uses. All of us involved with Jasmine can see her progressing so well in her physical and emotional recovery, and it is evident that she now shows trust and affection towards Kate. This process has taken time but has been worth the wait.

The following is in Kate's words:

It was a friend of mine who told me about Janine; she had seen her website and knew I was having problems with my mare, Jasmine. I thought, what have I got to lose? Jasmine was very unfriendly and could be difficult to handle at times. I was worried that she was going to be too much for me to cope with.

I had had Jasmine for about six months, but felt that she was putting up a barrier between me and her, one which I couldn't get through. She wouldn't let me in. We were growing further apart, but I couldn't understand why.

I wanted to know what was going on in her head, so when I read about Janine's abilities I was intrigued, and asked her to come out to meet Jasmine. I didn't know what to expect but kept an open mind – I told myself, just because you don't understand how or why something happens, doesn't mean it can't happen!

Janine started off with giving Jasmine some Reiki healing, which she took easily, relaxing and very obviously enjoying it. What I didn't understand until Janine started communicating with Jasmine was how emotional, opinionated and needy she was and is. Janine revealed to me how insecure Jasmine was about everything and how certain things really unsettled her. Once she was reassured that I was keeping her, and wanted to help her, the barriers fell away and she let me into her world.

For example, she said she wasn't happy with her feet, so now I keep her barefoot and bitless, and she is so much happier for it – her choice! There have been numerous other things she has revealed that I have been able to act upon to help her physically as well as mentally. Our relationship has blossomed for it. I keep our communications up as she is such a sensitive soul I don't want to let anything worry her to that point again.

Janine was also able to put Jasmine's mind at rest when I got Freddie, a youngster, as at first she was worried that she was being replaced by him, which wasn't the case. She and Freddie are now close, and it's obvious that they know they are 'brother and sister', even though they are kept in a large herd. After communicating with Freddie, Janine described his personality exactly and has told me all his funny little ways, including a few things he liked and some he wasn't keen on. It was so precise it gave me goosebumps – and that was a reading done from a photo.

I think Janine's animal communication is a valuable insight into animals' minds, giving humans the opportunity to work out how they can help make their animals' lives easier and more fulfilling.

Thank you so much for all your help with mine.

Jasmine and Kate

11

Orrick, the Welsh Cob

While I got over my relationship ending by doing up the semi-derelict house in Mid-Wales that I had purchased with help from family, I was also working on TV as a psychic via webcam. This was lovely, although quite odd; you never got to see the viewers or knew where they lived or anything. It was also exceptionally tiring 'tuning' into so many different energies.

I needed to build up my reputation here in this part of Wales, as a clairvoyant and as a horse and animal communicator and healer. Just one business card which I put out in the local health food shop advertising my readings got me call after call. Clients would come to the house for their readings, and one lady picked up my horse communication card to give to a friend. From that I received a call asking if I would go out and do a communication for a Welsh cob gelding called Orrick.

Orrick turned out to be some horse! The owners, a lovely couple called Sue and David, had bought him because they had been trekking, and had ridden him a few times, and wanted a quiet horse. Orrick was quite experienced; he had taken lots of people on lots of treks. He had seemed quiet to Sue and David and was sold as quiet. Well, within a week he turned into a total terror.

By now he wasn't in the slightest bit quiet; he loved standing on your feet, with a gleeful look on his face, and he ran the people ragged. He would drag them off when they tried to lead him, refusing to stand still for them to mount him, and once they were on his back and sitting in the saddle, when they asked him to move forward, he would either walk backwards or go so far, plant his feet and then turn for home, and no amount of pleading would help. Soon, his owners were at their wits' end, and I was their last resort.

When I first started to speak to Orrick he was really quite rude and wouldn't reply in any shape or form. So I offered him healing. He wasn't sure about this, but thought he would give it a try, and in fact he liked it.

He then opened up and told me that he wanted to return to the trekking centre that Sue and David had bought him from, as he liked the other horses there. Moreover, he missed his friend and the people who used to look after him. Since he had been purchased from a trekking centre, and these places don't always have the very best record for happy horses, I was totally surprised. Although most trekking centres look after their horses well, the horses have lots of different riders, and the varying ways of so many people can make them a bit unhappy. Plus not every person who rides them treats them with respect.

Anyway, a little hesitantly, I relayed this information to Sue and David. They asked me to ask him who his favourite horse friend was. He showed me a rather large fat cob who wasn't gifted with the best looks. His name was Sambo, or that is how it sounded to me.

Once my communication was finished, I didn't hear back from Sue and David for a few months. Then, out of the blue, I had a call to see if I would communicate with Orrick again.

When I arrived, I found there were two cobs there, and immediately I recognized Orrick's friend from the description he had given me. Indeed, he wasn't the best-looking horse, his head was rather large and his feet looked like they belonged to a shire, but he was a good sort. And his name was Rambo! I was very glad he didn't live up to his name.

This time, Orrick was very pleased to see me and asked for healing for himself and also for his friend. He introduced me to Rambo as 'the lady who talks like us', which I found quite a compliment.

Rambo was a real gentleman in all respects. And Orrick was like a different horse. I had to ask him, although I felt I knew the reason, why he had behaved so badly on my last visit. He did confirm that he thought that if he was bad, he would be taken back to the trekking centre – apparently it wouldn't have been the first time he had been sold and then sold right back again! But Sue and David were two very caring people who had gone out of their way to make Orrick happy. They had returned to the trekking centre to see if Sambo was there. After much discussion, they had negotiated a price for him, and as it was coming into winter and the treks were finished for that year, a deal was done.

The owners of the trekking centre very kindly offered to have both horses back again if it didn't work out, and they were interested to hear of Orrick's conversation with the 'horse lady'.

So now Orrick was happy, and Sue was enjoying taking David out on rides with her. I thought it was lovely that this couple was so concerned about their horse's wellbeing and his happiness that they had taken the trouble to go back to the centre, find his friend from not quite the right name, purchased him and brought him back with them. When Sue had only ever intended to buy one horse.

Many people ask me if anyone can speak to their horses and animals, and to be honest, most of us do so, all the time. All you need to do is learn to listen and to hear the messages you are being given.

Later on in the book, I will show you how to start communicating with your own animals.

12

Alice and Bunty

While cleaning the bottom field one day, my daughter and I noticed a lamb lying dead in the next field – or so it seemed. We immediately climbed over the fence to investigate. The poor animal was alive, but barely; it was hardly breathing and had no sense at all that we were there. My daughter Jayshea keeps sheep on her own farm thought this one might be too far gone to save, but we put some twigs over its face in an arc to protect it from crows trying to peck at its eyes, and we went home to ring the farmer. He said he would check on it later.

I kept thinking about the lamb. Two days later I was walking along the river on the other side of the field when I saw a lamb standing in the water with its head resting in it. The lamb from the other day was no longer there, and I was able to work out that this was the same animal now in the river and almost drowning. Luckily I had my friend Heather with me, and Heather being a lot more agile than me was able to climb the fence and lift the sheep over it.

We took her back home and rang the farmer, who said if we could save her, which he doubted, we could have her. We put her in the stable and made her comfortable lying down. She seemed totally paralysed. I tried feeding her with some milk but she seemed unable to move her mouth. In the end I had to carefully use a teaspoon.

My daughter came over and we bundled the sheep we called Alice into the car to take her to the vet. To be honest, the vet didn't give her much chance of survival; he thought that a type of bacterial meningitis had caused her paralysis. We were given some antibiotics and vitamins for her and then we took her home.

Typical symptoms of sheep meningitis include fever, neck rigidity and muscle spasms. The onset of symptoms can be slow or rapid. A lamb with meningitis often cannot stand, does not exhibit a suck reflex and appears weak and depressed. Unfortunately, the treatment of meningitis in sheep is often unsuccessful, with relapses common and the overall response being generally poor.

I started to give Alice Reiki healing throughout the day in sessions of five minutes. She just lay there. I decided to give her twenty-four hours. After that, I decided that if there was no improvement, I would take her back to the vet's to have her put to sleep. And to be honest, the vet didn't think she would last the night.

The next morning, Alice was still alive and her eyes flickered when she saw me. First, I gave her healing, then I worked the teat into her mouth. Her mouth was tight and she couldn't suck. Squeezing the teat, the milk slowly went in. I sat Alice up and held her, talked to her and sent her healing. All the while her eyes watched me.

Twenty-four hours later, I couldn't make the decision to put her down. By now she was starting to swallow more milk but still couldn't suck.

Every day, I carried Alice round to the garden to lie on the grass and get some sun. The dogs would lie near her. After I propped her up, she would watch all the goings on. We carefully poked small amounts of grass into her mouth and I concentrated the healing on her head and her mouth. The first time she chewed was lovely to see, and then, two weeks later, she stood up on her own.

When Alice attempted to eat she would have her head almost touching her side and would move round in endless circles. We had to pull the grass up for her and poke it into the side of her mouth. After two months she was physically stronger but still not eating unaided; she would pull at the grass but nothing would go in. I began to worry what would happen in the future when she was fully grown, wondering how I would manage to feed her then. Then, one day, she took the grass from my outstretched hand and ate it herself. Her head was still at an odd angle, and I would sit with her on my lap, gently massaging her head and neck to straighten it. By now, Alice was having Reiki regularly, would follow the dogs quite happily and look up when her name was called. In the winter, she spent time in her stable.

At times, though, Alice would go dead still and her eyes would be glassy, as if someone had switched the lights out. When she was like this, she would stay in a trance. It was only through us

50

constantly calling her name that it was possible for her to come out of it.

When Alice was two years old, my daughter Jayshea asked me if I would take a lamb as a friend for her. He was what you call a 'meat lamb' – i.e. he was due to go off for market – but Jayshea couldn't bring herself to send him as, although he wasn't hand-reared, he was super friendly and was well known by all the visitors to her farm. He was in the habit of gently bunting people, which had gained him the name Bunty.

Bunty duly arrived, and unsurprisingly, Alice didn't bother with him. Unsurprising because although she had been brought up with sheep for the first month of her life had, since coming to live with me, mixed with humans and dogs and horses instead. Occasionally, Alice would look at the sheep in the field surrounding us, and on the odd time that they came into our field, she would head for her stable. The other sheep would follow her, then stand back looking in amazement at this strange sheep, not only going up to humans but letting them stroke her.

So Alice took one look at Bunty and set off to do her own thing. Bunty, however, clung to Alice like glue. While he was busy eating some tasty grass, Alice would slip away and ignore his frantic calls. Eventually, Bunty would find her with our help. The first time that they were sheared together, Bunty sat all day by her discarded fleece; he didn't recognize the clipped Alice and, in fact, when he did see her, he ran off.

A year or so down the line, the two sheep have become firm friends. Alice is now three. Even now, at times, the 'lights go out', just not as often. It is lovely to see her skipping about like a lamb. The meningitis has made her quite retarded and she is nothing like a normal sheep.

Bunty loves the fuss of visitors to the house, who in turn love to stroke him. He is addicted to horse sweets, so much so that he chases after you if he smells them in your pockets – no joke now that he is a fully grown and rather large animal, so he is only given them on occasion.

Alice, though, is aloof with strangers but comes as soon as I call her. When she heads down the river path I have to go and fetch her back as she forgets where she is and will stand calling until I find her. She also gets caught up in the tape for electric fencing, walks through hedges and does not have any sense of danger. She usually comes in at nights covered all over in brambles, looking like the sheep we drew as children, with a round body, fluffed-up coat from the burrs and stick-thin legs. She is lovely to have and adores having her face stroked. I am so glad that I persevered with her.

Alice and Bunty

13

Paul the Psychic Octopus

In September 2010, I was contacted by a man called Alexandre Philippe on email. He had read about me and thought I would be the ideal psychic to do a reading for an octopus called Paul as he and his team were making a documentary about him.

I must admit to being surprised (and it did cross my mind that it might be a hoax), but in no time at all I was speaking to Alexandre on the phone and arrangements were being made for the film-makers to come to my house to film me doing a reading for Paul. This was after speaking to my son Ashley, who informed me that Paul was indeed a psychic octopus who had correctly predicted the outcome of eight matches of the 2010 World Cup, including the final. I checked out Google and glanced at a little bit more about him before I stopped reading. I didn't want what I'd read to influence me in any way.

After some delays, Alexandre and his cameraman arrived. They had come from America via a journey across Europe, including Germany, where Paul lived, and other various people in connection with the documentary. The living room was set up with lights and they opened up a picture of Paul on their laptop so that I could focus on it while doing the reading. The filming started.

I had done communications before for birds and lizards but never an octopus. Tuning into Paul, I immediately received a series of emotions and feelings. All the time I was reading for him, he was communicating with me and sending me healing.

Paul explained to me that he was psychic – although as he wasn't sure of the words, this was explained in feelings. He showed me the aura, and explained that he was able to read the energy from this. While he had absolutely no idea what football was, he knew when asked which team would win. He also told me he wasn't the only octopus that could do this. And, after they had stopped filming, they told me that people in Germany were training another octopus to work psychically. They didn't go into detail and I didn't ask.

I asked Paul where he was born. Obviously, I wasn't expecting him to name the place, but he did give me the description, and he showed me a white beach and warm seas. So I guessed he had come from somewhere in the southern Mediterranean, like Italy or Greece.

I was asked to ask him if he would like to retire, and so I showed him as best I could what I meant. For his answer, Paul said he wanted just to relax now and enjoy the life he had left. From what he said I had the feeling that he would die sooner than he perhaps should. I asked him what he would like to make him happy and he gave me shellfish and said that he needed to procreate.

I then got an overwhelming feeling of sadness as I understood he was telling me that his life was ending. I tried hard to stop the tears from flowing – I was wearing my usual black eye make-up, not a good sight on film! I sent love and healing to Paul, and he sent love back to me. When I looked into his eyes in his photo it was as if he was a person, and to this day I cannot say what came over me.

I was asked to ask Paul other questions, but due to channelling the information I cannot remember what was said – only this overwhelming feeling of sadness. I asked him if he was happy, and he said he was. He liked the people doing the filming and said that one of them had put his hand in the water and he had wrapped his tentacle around it. Alexandre confirmed this, and also thought there was something special about Paul.

Paul asked if he could see me, and I replied that I would come in the New Year. Paul was unsure what I meant by the New Year, and once I'd managed to show him in my own way the concept of the time, he seemed sad and said it would be too late. I didn't understand what he meant by this as he was only two years old and octopuses live to be three, and I had been invited over to Germany the next year to see him and be filmed with him.

Two weeks after the filming, Paul was dead. Sadly I never did get to meet him. He was right, time ran out. But I will always be thankful I was given the chance to speak to him. For people who doubt or find it difficult to understand how you can communicate with a creature from a totally different species, I would say this: remember that everything is energy and it is the energy they are giving off that I am reading. It does not have a language, it is universal. That is how we psychics read for people.

Was Paul psychic? I would have to answer a resounding yes. He was also very special. He told me that there were lots like him in the oceans who could do this, and we humans will one day believe it.

I hope we believe sooner rather than later.

Paul the Octopus

14

Tia and Cheryl

Cheryl contacted me via email as she wanted a reading for her lovely horse Tia. She gave me Tia's age and also sent a picture. As soon as I linked into Tia I got the wow factor. She is a star and she knows it! She has an energy field that is very drawing to people, and she is a horse that always gets a second look. This is not so much to do with looks as to do with her presence, although she is lovely looking too.

One of the very first things that Tia said to me was that she was a fussy eater, and that she also loved having very clean troughs and buckets to eat and drink out of. She also told me that her owner Cheryl did indeed keep her implements nice and clean – and I don't think a horse has ever told me this before! Tia told me that she mirrors Cheryl, which was affecting Tia's method of moving. She told me that her owner sat slightly to one side, but that she compensates for her. This appeared to make Tia look unlevel at times. She told me that she did show-jumping and when Cheryl lost her focus, she lost hers. This was confirmed by Cheryl.

Tia said that she picked up on Cheryl's moods and can get edgy when her owner feels nervous, even stopping at a particular jump if she picked up that her owner was anxious about a daunting hedge or a difficult height.

Tia had quite an opinion on things, but in a nice way; she told me that her owner didn't listen to her own thoughts or have her own ideas but went along with other people's instead. Tia wanted Cheryl to trust both herself and her horse more. Cheryl confirmed to me that she tends to ask others what she should do rather than going with her own intuition. And that in addition she feels inadequate at times, so needs confirmation that she is doing things OK. I think Cheryl was very pleased, though, to learn that Tia had told me she was very happy with her as her partner.

Tia showed me images of herself being spooky and full of life. She also admitted to me that she did get nervous sometimes and it wasn't always Cheryl who made her nervous. About this, I suggested to Cheryl that she showed her horse lots of different situations that might spook her, with the intention that when she came across them in future she was no longer nervous of them. Cheryl thought this was a good idea.

Tia also told me of another horse that was around – but was in spirit. She wanted Cheryl to know this.

There was some stiffness showing in Tia's neck; I recommended carrot stretches for removing this. Cheryl confirmed that Tia had been seeing 'the back man' quite regularly to sort this out. Although a confident horse, Tia came over as an animal that did need a leader and prefers not to be in charge. In a herd of horses, she would be the second mare.

She was very specific about colours to me and mentioned a blue stable rug and also a purple spray which she hated and doesn't want on again, thank you very much. Flies are on Tia's most hated list, and where some horses can put up with them, she cannot and needs protection. She told me that she had a fly rug and although at times it made her hot, she preferred it to the flies.

Tia told me lots more detail about her life and how she likes it. She feels well in herself and is a happy horse; she likes to go out in the field but doesn't mind a stable, although it seemed that this was not always the case. She enjoys some hacking out but not so much on her own since she lacks confidence. I felt that with Cheryl taking the lead, Tia would be much better at this in future. She had been very difficult to ride and said she was so glad that Cheryl had stuck with her. She needed confirmation that she would stay with Cheryl as she was insecure about her past and was afraid of having to move homes.

I was able to reassure Tia that she wouldn't be sold – it can happen that owners have good intentions and say they will keep their horses but then they don't, however, in this case Cheryl was adamant that Tia was staying. Once Tia took this in, the barriers fell away and she was able to feel safe.

Cheryl's words
I had spent three years working on my mare Tia. During that time she had changed from being impossible to ride to going quite well. But there were a few things that were holding us back and I couldn't

put my finger on it. I contacted Janine in the hope that maybe she could provide some insight and help us put the last few things together.

The communication that I received back from Tia through Janine was so accurate and informative – Tia keeps her feed bucket and water drinker immaculately clean, and here it was, one of the first things she told Janine, that she liked to eat and drink out of clean things! Our communication was worth every penny, as I was encouraged to respond and ask more questions.

Cheryl and Tia.

Tia and I now have a bond and it has reached an incredible depth; we have moved up two height grades in our jumping and I have no doubt that we will move again before the end of the year.

I understand Tia, and she now knows that she is safe with me, and to have that communicated in a way that she understands is priceless. Horses understand us more than we understand them, so it's nice to have someone you can turn to who can give you some more insight. Janine is a lovely person and is always willing to help.

Thank you, Janine.

15

Sam and Elfie Sprout Wings

Before I start I'd just like to clarify a couple of things. Firstly, I share the same first name as the author of this book, so from now on I will refer to myself as J9, so as not to confuse anyone. Secondly, Sam and Elfie didn't literally sprout wings.

For many years, my husband had been hankering after living abroad, and in December 2009 it actually happened. I will pick up the story from January 2009, when we initially thought we were moving to Canada. At that time, I owned five horses, of which three were rehab/rescue horses. Also then, I was unaware of Janine Wilbraham, and I was using another animal communicator.

The relevance of this is that all five horses were asked if they wanted to come with us or stay in the UK. And to that question came the answer that Sam (who was my first ever horse) was the only one who asked to come – in fact, what he actually said was that I had promised I would never leave him, and he wanted to hold me to that promise. This is true, and he is the only horse I have ever said it to. I would also like to point out that at this stage I wasn't sure if I could afford to take any of them.

We soon discovered that our destination was to be New Zealand rather than Canada. This changed everything as flights for horses to New Zealand were considerably more expensive. Efforts were made to rehome all five horses. Three were successfully rehomed (my sister had one and my best friend took two, meaning they could stay together). The two horses remaining were Sam and Elfie. Sam, being autistic, needs very special handling, while Elfie was the first youngster I had ever worked with (backing included), so I had a fondness for them both. However, I also felt I had a duty to try and rehome them and not put them through the great stress of such a move.

Sam's trial home was perfect, the lady who had him was the best I could have wished for, but sadly she just wasn't me and he couldn't handle it, so after a week he came home (this communication I heard myself, loud and clear).

Elfie also went out on loan, with a view to buy, to a gentleman I knew very well and with whom I used to hunt. Let's call him Mr X. Now, this is where I made my first mistake, because I thought that Elfie, with all his youth and bravado, was a tough cookie and could deal with change. Here, I would like to tell you that my horses are all barefoot, live out 24/7, are on grain- and sugar-free diets, are ridden in WOW™ saddles and are handled using natural horsemanship methods.

Anyway, the day I dropped Elfie off at his new home with Mr X, I went out for a ride with his new owner's daughter, on her father's horse, while she rode Elfie. As we walked out of the stable, Mr X's horse played up a bit, resulting in Mr X getting cross with her. I watched as Elfie lifted his head in surprise and backed up. I should have taken Elfie home there and then: mistake number two.

This now takes me to the point where Janine comes in. Two days later, I discovered that when Mr X had tacked Elfie up the following day, Elfie had bitten him. I was mortified when I found out, and when I questioned Mr X about what had happened he said that it was nothing and he was all right. That was when I pointed out that I wasn't worried about him, I wanted to know what he had done to my horse to cause Elfie to want to bite him, as he had never bitten anyone before.

I had already been working with Janine, in trying to find Elfie a new home, so when I rang her she took my call immediately. She wanted to communicate with Elfie and find out what exactly had happened. Janine's description of Mr X via Elfie was scarily accurate, even though Janine had never met him. This was the reading:

Janine – Elfie, why did you bite Mr X?

Elfie – He barged into the stable, was disrespectful and didn't ask.

– He's not right for me (something I should have realized from day one).

– He's fast and impatient.

– He's brusque with me.

– My back is sore.

– Mr X doesn't give me time to think.

– Mr X is rush, rush, rush, head in a whirl.

– I feel like I'm being bossed around.

– Mr X is not careful putting my saddle on, he's hurried and terse.

– I don't like Mr X's energy.

Elfie

There was a lot more to the reading but this was the nuts and bolts of it, and while I can't prove any of it, I do know Mr X extremely well, and this description of him was incredibly accurate.

So, to cut a long story short, Elfie was brought home and I announced to my husband that both Sam and Elfie were emigrating with us on the grounds that Sam needed Elfie to help get him through the journey. Thankfully, I have a very understanding husband.

The next stage of the operation involved leaving both Sam and Elfie in the careful hands of my dear friend Michelle and her daughter Emily. Michelle works with autistic children and also has an autistic son, Brian, who can be very loud and boisterous sometimes. I needed to make sure both horses were happy being left with Michelle and family for six months while we set up home in New Zealand.

Coincidentally, up till then we had only suspected for a long time that Sam was also autistic, and a reading with Janine confirmed this:

> Janine – Sam, will you be OK left with Michelle looking after you? (It hadn't been decided then if he would go, until Sam told us himself.)
>
> Sam – I'm unhappy, unsure of what is to happen to me. I don't understand why they have to go.
>
> – I will be OK as long as it's done gradually and J9 doesn't suddenly disappear.
>
> – Michelle and family have to treat me in the same way that J9 does.
>
> Janine – Can you handle Brian?
>
> Sam – I don't like his shouting, but I do have an affinity with him because we are alike!

The rest of the reading was all about Sam's personality, which was all very true, but I won't bore you with it here.

We did as Sam had requested and we set up the handover very slowly. Michelle learnt to handle Sam as I do (which came easy to her, because of her background experience), and Sam coped with all the changes far better than I could have imagined.

I had another communication with Janine to make sure that both horses were happy and aware of what was about to take place. Elfie was excited about the adventure and happy to get on with it, but Sam was sad as he didn't want Michelle and Emily to think he didn't like them. He also asked if Elfie could lead the way, especially when getting into trucks. Elfie was happy with this, so the transport company was given strict instructions to lead Elfie first. (This proved to be a very successful move as no problems were incurred.

And I would like to point out that if Sam ever chooses not to load, nothing you can do will change his mind.)

Sam

During this reading it was agreed that Janine would stay in contact with the two horses before and throughout the journey to New Zealand, which was to take two days. She also checked in with them when they were in quarantine.

After we had been in New Zealand for a couple of months and the horses were still in the UK, I had a reading with Janine for myself. Before Janine had got started, Elfie barged his way into her thoughts and wanted to know if I was all right and to ask when they were joining me. Cheeky monkey!

Apart from a delay of one week which was spent in the UK because of the volcanic activity in Iceland affecting so many flights, the boys arrived safely in New Zealand at their new home just after my birthday in May. Another communication with Janine provided the following information:

Janine – How do you feel after your long trip?

Answer – Their feet and the backs of their legs were sore. (By the time they arrived, their feet were grown horrendously long and needed some major trimming. The ligaments and tendons up the backs of their legs were causing the soreness.)

– They both showed concern at the length of the journey, and the extra week's delay in the UK had caused them quite a bit of stress.

Janine – Why are you bullying Nemisha (a pony we had rescued just before they arrived)?

Answer – They were jealous of her and said she talked funny (well, she is a Kiwi!). Janine said they would all settle down within two weeks, and they did.

– They said they felt insecure and needed me to tell them they were staying – so I did.

Elfie – What's that funny-smelling stuff you're putting in my feed and what's it for?

Answer – I'd been putting B-complex in their food to help with the stress.

The rest of the conversation was about Elfie asking for healing, saying where he needed it and where he would like me to proceed next with his work. He also remembered to say 'thank you' to Janine for saving him from that awful man Mr X, which I found quite funny as I can't imagine Janine remembering her communications with that kind of detail.

The interesting thing to note was that Sam, who we thought was going to be the biggest casualty of the trip, was absolutely flourishing, whereas Elfie, who had been big, strong and tough about the idea, was having a hard time. This had been my third mistake: we had been so worried about Sam that we had put all our energies into him, neglecting poor Elfie.

After four months in New Zealand, Elfie still wasn't quite right, wasn't himself, so we arranged another communication with Janine. It went like this:

Question – Is there anything you would like to tell us?

Answer – He feels out of sorts, his guts are stressed,* he is feeling nervous and fearful. And he needed to tell us he is five now!

– He thinks we are moving again and that he is going on another long journey.**

– He is still emotionally recovering from the journey and is sensitive to people's energies (he quickly reminded us both of Mr X – again!)

– He has been getting headaches (dehydration).***

Question – Why are you so bossy in the trailer?

Answer – He thinks the other horse is going to pinch his hay and he needs more room.****

Question – How do your feet feel with the new trim we are trying?

Answer – Tingly, feels different, but not in a bad way.*****

*I have recently found out that the pasture my horses are on here in New Zealand can cause lots of problems with their guts, with increased anxiety, physical and emotional stress and several other symptoms which Elfie is displaying. We are in the process of trying him on some special supplements to help with this until we can sort the grass out.

**We will be moving again, unfortunately, as we are living in rented until we can find somewhere. I have told both horses it will not be a long journey.

***Their water trough is away from the field they graze in, to encourage movement. The problem is that Elfie is so insecure he hasn't wanted to go for a drink on his own, so we give him a drink when he comes in for his breakfast and his tea and he seems better for it. I am hoping that once the supplements detox him from the nasty grass, he will start going to drink on his own again.

****I'd had a bad experience with Sam spooking and jumping over the breast bar in the trailer, so I had shortened up both the travelling stalls so they couldn't step back to make the jump. I've since lengthened Elfie's at his request, and he's travelling much more quietly. Sadly, there is nothing I can do about the hay thief!

*****All my horses are now being trimmed using the Strasser Method (barefoot-only hoof care – don't knock it until you've thoroughly investigated it). They claim it increases circulation in the foot – I expect that would be the tingling he was experiencing.

Sam also had a communication that day. He said:

    – His feet felt more springy and he noticed that his heels had been lowered (they had).

    – The backs of his legs were stiff.*

    – He felt very well and bright, and had recovered from the journey.

    – When asked if he wanted to compete, he said no thank you, that he was happy doing what he was doing, babysitting and all.**

*By lowering his heels, the backs of his legs would be tight, just like taking off high heels after spending an evening dancing.

**Sam has been given a new job since coming to NZ, and that is riding out with a youngster we bought over here to keep him company, and being on lead when I ride Elfie out to keep him company – in other words . . . babysitting the new youngster.

While Elfie still isn't quite right after his long journey, I believe he would have been a lot worse if it were not for Janine's excellent communication skills. I also believe that Sam would probably have never made it at all.

Communication is a dying art. Most people struggle to communicate with someone who speaks the same language, never mind across species. I have used animal communicators for over a decade now and their advice has always been invaluable. I believe my horses lead happier lives because of it, and I don't believe I could successfully have transported two horses from Cornwall to New Zealand, when I was already living on the other side of the world, without the help of Michelle and her family and Janine and her excellent communication skills.

Janine thinks Elfie will be much better come October 2010. I think that now this new information about the grass has come to light, he will be back to his old self in no time.

Thank you, Janine, for being so good at what you do.

J9 Burns, Sam and Elfie (New Zealand).

16

How to Communicate with your Own Horse or Animal

When people come to my workshops to learn how to communicate, the first part of the day is spent tuning into their intuition and starting to pick up information. It is not true that only the gifted few can do this; we are all born with the ability to listen, and some can talk to animals as children, but as we grow up we are told we are being fanciful and warned not to be silly, and so we start to lose that talent. Remember, though, that age is not an issue in learning to communicate; we can learn at any age up until we leave the earth plane, and in this chapter I am going to teach you how.

Animal communication has been around for many hundreds of years. In the past it was seen as normal by some cultures to speak to their animals, for example shamans used to speak to their totem animals. When you think about it, we all, every day, do talk to our dogs and our cats and our other animals as if they are people.

Remember, every living thing gives off energy in their auric field, the auric field being the electromagnetic field that is unique to each individual. Information is held in it, and thoughts are energy too. You can try an experiment with your pet; if you have a dog, think into your mind without making any move, do they want to go for a walk? Try it a couple of times and you will see, they will read your thoughts.

The only thing you need is an open heart and love, and of course to believe the information that is coming through to you. So listen and believe. Before you move on to learning how to communicate, though, you need to know how to get yourselves ready in your mind and in your energy levels, which means slowing things down a little and relaxing.

So let's start: which means no alcohol or recreational drugs while you are meditating or communicating; you want a clear mind. Pour yourself some nice clear water, take the phone off the hook and find somewhere where you can sit quietly without being disturbed. Put on some soothing music without words to set the mood. Don't wear constricting clothing, and sit comfortably with your feet on the floor. You can lie down, but be aware, you may fall asleep!

Now, with your hands folded loosely in your lap, I want you to count your breathing in – one, two, three, four – and your breathing out. Don't hyperventilate, just breathe in and out. In, count one, two, three, four. Breathe out, one, two, three, four. This is called the four-fold breath. This way of breathing changes your brainwaves, making you more relaxed. You can do this in your bath, shower, garden, wherever – although not while driving or operating machinery. Try to do this for at least ten minutes. Don't worry if thoughts come into your head, just let go of them and over time it will get easier to keep them at bay while you count one, two, three, four . . . Slowly bring your breathing back into the present. This was your first meditation.

There are many more different ones you can do, but this will get you started. It can help lower your blood pressure and it can help prolong your life. Don't try and over meditate at first but build it up gradually; it won't hurt you, though, and you shouldn't be in competition with other people who are meditating. Some people meditate for an hour or more each day. Do what you prefer.

On the subject of visualization while meditating, many people think they are unable to visualize but everyone can in fact do it. Try thinking about your kettle in your kitchen, where it is located and what is near to it, and there you are, you have visualized. A visualization meditation is different to the breathing one. In this you go on a journey (do read about shamanic meditations), perhaps seeing yourself in a beautiful garden, smelling the flowers, hearing the birds, and then sitting on a bench, where you sit to meditate and let whatever come through.

Breathing around Animals
Most of us breathe far too shallowly. Horses and other animals respond to people who breathe slowly, which lowers your energy, sending oxygen to your muscles and allowing tightness and tension to leave your body. You can breathe like this whenever you are

around horses and stressed animals. By regulating my breathing, all animals will allow me to be close to them, even garden birds. Try also the six-fold breath, where you breathe in to a count of six and out to a count of six.

Breathing with Your Horse

When you are doing the four-fold or six-fold breath comfortably, try doing it with your horse. Stand next to your horse and monitor his breathing by looking at his tummy. Put your hand on his back and begin to breathe in the same pattern as your horse. After a few minutes, slow your breathing down, inviting your horse to follow you with his breathing. If he doesn't follow you (and sometimes this can happen), return to following his breathing again. It's not a big issue; practice, as they say, makes perfect, so don't give up.

Starting to Communicate

The first step to take with your horse, dog or other animal is:

a) not to talk too much; your equine and canine friends don't spend hours in long verbal conversations with each other, and

b) be open to receiving the information; sometimes it can be difficult for us to believe what we are hearing, and we don't trust our ability.

Get yourself a picture of your horse or animal and place it in front of you. Using photographs is the same as having the animal there in front of you but with fewer distractions.

Breathe in from your chest and breathe out, letting your mind slow down a little, and relax. Look at the photo, let the thoughts come to you; ask your question and wait for the answer. This is the start of learning a new skill, and remember, as humans we are used to verbal communication and our own skills relating to that. This is different.

Don't ask a really important question at first, ask something simple like, do you like your food? Then just listen. This can be hard for us to do, but you must if you want to be successful. For now, it will be too early to sort out and decide what are your own thoughts and what are messages that you are receiving, but don't worry, it will soon become apparent. You may get the answer hours or days later;

71

remember, you are just starting out. Animal communication is the most basic form of communication, and like a muscle, it becomes better with use.

So how do I ask questions, and what happens next? I start with asking the horse or animal basic questions, and I receive from them words, pictures, thoughts or emotions – sometimes the whole lot! If I ask if they have any pain, they will show me in an area of my body that most corresponds to theirs, for example their back leg, my leg; their front leg, my arm. Sometimes they show me themselves moving, so I can see the lame area. They may tell me how the injury happened, but always remember, they cannot diagnose illness. Only a qualified vet can do that. The information you receive will be pure and untainted by outside influences, and there are not any bad horses or animals, only those that have been made that way by humans.

Some animals are natural comedians and some prefer to remain stoic at all costs, fearful of letting go in case they are let down again. This can happen to a lot of rescue animals, but not all. Each animal has its own personality and is an individual; they are here for a purpose. If you are reading this book, you no doubt care for horses and animals, and want to help them, so thank you.

One thing to remember always: horses and animals are incredibly sensitive to the energies around them, so in order to communicate with them we need to be aware of the mental images in our minds. When we are afraid, we can confuse animals terribly. They pick up on our fear and then act on it.

How many of us have started to get ready to go to a show and found the horse won't load into the lorry or trailer? Or suddenly we feel nervous and the horse goes all silly. And if you feel cross or angry over something entirely unrelated to your animal, they will pick up on it. So what do you do? Breathe. Breathe yourself calm for a few seconds or minutes, take time out and let your body balance itself.

What blocks communication
There are a number of reasons why communication can be blocked: being out of touch with your own physical body, or emotional blocks. Emotional blocks are where you might have a lot of

emotional issues still; for example, you might have lost a pet and still be feeling quite raw about it, or you could be having relationship problems that make you more emotional, and so you are not able to free the heart chakra. And sometimes the information being 'received' may be incorrect – it might be that you are thinking up what you want to hear. Or the information coming through can be hard to take and upsetting. To prevent communication from being blocked, it is important to train and practise and put your feelings to one side.

I believe, however, that the most common block to communication is expectation. The media portrays psychics and clairvoyants as receiving vivid descriptions, and yes, some do, but not all. It is possible you may not see things but hear them into your head or have feelings. Learn to trust them – but don't add to them.

Approaching a horse or other animal to communicate with them

How you approach an animal – either by photograph or in person – is very important. If you are there in person, stand back, let them come to you and sniff you, it is their version of a handshake. Let them into your space rather than force yourself into theirs. Once they have accepted you, then you can place a hand on their body. Try not to go for their head at first, unless they are a dog; for horses, the back shoulder area is best.

Dogs do like their head rubbed, so they can be touched there. If it is safe to do so, close your eyes for a few seconds, slow your breathing and let go of any thoughts that may invade you. Tell the animal in your mind (remembering that all thoughts are energy and can be picked up) what you are about to do; use your own words but not too many, let it flow, ask a simple question then wait for the answer, tell them they will be safe with you. Never punish an animal for speaking the truth. If you think you wouldn't like to hear a particular answer, then don't ask the question!

The information may come quite slowly or quite fast, remember animals don't speak to us like we do to each other. You may get feelings and get very emotional, so do be aware, and it may change for ever how you see horses and other animals. Make sure you are ready for this.

Always, at the end of a communication, thank them, and if you are a healer, offer healing to them. The next chapter will show you how to heal your own animals.

One final word: above all else, NEVER MAKE PROMISES YOU CANNOT KEEP.

17

How to Heal

To do any healing, you have to be quiet, calm and not under the influence of any drink or recreational drugs. Most prescription drugs are OK but if you are on antidepressant drugs it is advisable to ask your doctor first. Ideally, it is best to eat a low-vibration food, i.e. something which isn't meat-based, but this is not compulsory. However, over time you may find yourself leaning that way in any case. Please refer to the previous chapter on communicating with your own animals in which I describe how to meditate.

So once you are relaxed, I want you to slow your breathing. What will help greatly is to learn how to open your chakras, the wheels of energy located in the body. Opening them can help with healing as well as communication. I always start at the crown chakra – although many people start at the root chakra, so feel free to reverse this order if you wish.

Starting with your crown, imagine a lovely light cream rosebud. Turn it slowly so that it opens up into a beautiful full-blown rose.

Now move down to your third eye chakra. This is located in the centre of your forehead. I want you to picture an indigo colour rosebud and turn it, too, until you see a lovely full-blown rose.

Move down to your throat chakra. See a blue rosebud and turn it, watching it become a fully blown rose.

Your heart chakra is next. This is green – or pink if you wish. Turn this rosebud until it opens into a full-blown rose.

Now move down to your solar plexus, which is the top part of your stomach. Here I want you to visualize a yellow rosebud and turn it so that it opens into a beautiful fully blown flower.

Below this is your sacral plexus, below the belly button. Here picture an orange rosebud. Turn it, too, until it becomes a full-blown rose.

And finally, below this is your root chakra, otherwise known as your base chakra, which lies at the base of your spine. Visualize here a beautiful red rosebud, and turn it so that it becomes a full-blown flower.

Your chakras are now open and you are ready to proceed. Once you become more adept at it you can do a faster opening, imagining a series of trap doors opening for you.

Now you can imagine a bright white or cream light coming down into your crown and heart chakra. Allow it to travel down into your heart, down through your chest, and let it flow through your hands. It will take a couple of seconds, but once it has started it is a bit like turning on a hosepipe. Ask in your head for the healing to flow, and it will.

Practise, if you wish, on a friend or partner. They will feel the energy. Then, if you feel ready, ask permission of your horse or animal to practise healing on them. This is important. If they walk off, they are saying no, so please respect this; you can always try another day. Put your hands on your horse or animal and let the healing flow. Usually the neck or the back is the best place to start.

Once the healing is over, the animal may walk away and have a drink or go to the toilet. Thank the energy source and the animal, then think the healing off. Remember, the horse or animal should not be worked after the healing, and they may sleep a lot more that day. And there it is. You can also use it on yourself as well; follow the above and lay your hands on your own body. You will find that as you get better, animals will come to you for healing.

If you would like to get into healing or practise it as a profession, then do train with someone who offers Reiki and is registered with a recognized body.

One thing to remember: please do not give healing unless you have permission from the animal or person first.

18
Telyn and Annette

I was asked to go out to see Telyn on a recommendation due to her being stiff and at times uncomfortable and also Annette, her owner, wished to see what she would say when she was communicated with. She had never had this done before so was quite intrigued.

When I arrived at the livery yard where she was kept, Telyn was in her stable waiting, and what a beautiful pony she was; her coat shone, she looked the picture of health, if a little bit rotund! She was 21 at the time and did not look her age at all.

Whilst speaking with her I offered her healing which she accepted gratefully but, of course, this being Telyn, I had to tell her what healing was, and what she would feel. She indicated that she had pain in her one shoulder, though she refused to have hands on healing, so, keeping my hands off, I directed healing that way. The next visit she let me touch the shoulder and enjoyed the hands on healing.

Telyn was a very chatty horse and spoke of lots of things. She liked her owner, Annette, and was happy with her. She told me of the old horse called Rob she shared her field with and how at times he was stiff and would I give him some healing, which I did before I left the yard. She also told me that he twittered on a bit and said, "But so does his owner!" This made me and Annette laugh as this was just what she was doing. She did not really believe all the stories that Rob told her as, according to him, he had done lots of things in his life and won lots of rosettes; although she liked him she found he was a bit full of himself at times. But she did tell me that he pulled a cart and his owner sat on it. This she found odd at first with the noise but soon got used to it when they went out together.

Telyn told me that before Annette owned her, she had gone to lots of shows and won rosettes, and when I asked her did she enjoy it, she gave me such a look and said of course she did and when was Annette taking her? I asked her what she liked most about the shows and she told me people praised her and lots came to talk to her, which she loved. She really is a horse that loves attention.

She didn't like being in the indoor school though and said she did not like going in endless circles and became immensely fed up with it, to this Annette agreed.

Annette asked about hacking out and she was very informative describing the hills and things around her. She liked going to different places. She did, though, prefer going out with other horses. She also described a place that Annette recognised from a few weeks previously that they had boxed to. Telyn said she remembered it from years ago, and it seemed that at one time with a previous owner she had been there as she lived not far from the ride. Annette confirmed that this was correct.

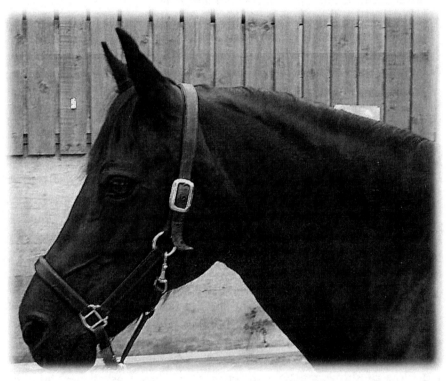

Telyn

When I asked Telyn about any pain that she may have, Telyn told me that she ached a bit around her back legs and hips, and her foot hurt. Horses cannot diagnose any illness; they are like us in that way we know something may hurt but don't know why until we see a doctor, it is the same with horses, but they will say where the pain is and also give the feelings of the pain to the communicator. It was later found, after x-rays had been taken, that she had a dropped pedal bone due to laminitis, this has now been sorted out with shoeing and treatment from the vet. She was also treated for her arthritis. She is now back in light work and feeling full of herself.

On the latest visit with her she told me that she did not like the injections and that they hurt. I tried to explain that it would make her better as it was helping her arthritis and she would not have any more now, she seemed okay with this. She was feeling much better in herself as well and the aches had gone. She also showed me herself cantering and when I asked Annette she admitted that she had broken into a canter on a ride and enjoyed herself, although she is still meant to be in walk most of the time.

I always enjoy visiting Telyn as she is so funny and even when I don't visit, if I have not been for a while, she will communicate with me asking when I am coming over to see her.

19

Smurf the Collie Cross

I was contacted by a lovely lady to see if I would communicate with her dog Smurf, she had him for a week and he was a rescue dog. Smurf was only approximately eight months old but had already had two homes and had come into the rescue centre as a last attempt to get him a home he would stay in. His previous owners had found him too difficult to live with as he would chew things up and not stay on his own. And now he was not settling with Jane and she was concerned that he would not eat or drink. Jane was feeling very depressed about this. She had had the dog three days and no food or water had passed his lips. She had contacted the vet, who said when he was hungry he would eat, but so far this hadn't happened.

As Jane lived over a hundred miles from me I suggested a phone reading for Smurf, although she was prepared to drive him over to me if needed.

I asked for a photograph to be sent via email so I could use it to speak with him, and we arranged a time for her to ring me; I don't need the animal there while doing a reading as long as I have a picture to see.

At the appointed time Jane rang me up and straight away as I looked at the picture, information started coming through from the dog. Jane said he was looking at her rather strangely as I was speaking to him.

I asked Smurf some basic questions about where he lived and who with. He told me that he thought the house was nice, and that he had a lovely basket with a soft blanket in, that it was in the kitchen and it was warm, he had been in the garden, and that a cat lived with them who slept all the time. Jane confirmed the information that he gave me.

Then I asked Smurf if he was hungry and he said yes. I asked if he was thirsty, showing him in my mind a bowl of water, again he said yes. Then I asked him why he didn't drink his water. He went very quiet and stopped speaking to me. So I asked about the cat and he spoke about him, saying he was a nice cat and he got up to eat then went back to sleep; he had tried speaking to the cat but as he was always sleeping it was difficult. I then asked Smurf about his food and why he didn't eat. At first he went quiet, then he showed me someone kicking out at him while he was eating his dinner and also a lot of noise. As Smurf spoke to me I passed this on to Jane, and we could not understand why this was, since from what she had been told Smurf's previous owners were very pleasant and had a nice home but didn't get on with his chewing. And so again I asked about the water and again Smurf showed me him being shouted at while he was drinking.

Jane was feeling terrible about this, she was concerned that I might think it was she who had done this to him, but I knew that it wasn't.

While I was on the phone talking to Smurf Jane fetched him some water and I encouraged him to drink. Within minutes he was drinking. He did look worried, Jane said, but as she sat and stroked him he calmed down and drank and drank. Next, we tried it with his food and it worked; at first he snatched a bit then ran away from his dish, cowering, but with me communicating and Jane stroking him, Smurf finished off his first meal since Jane had had him. Jane was elated that he was OK and the next day she rang me to say that he had curled up on her lap and slept for over two hours without moving.

Smurf has settled very well now into his new home and although we can never prove what happened with his previous home, Jane did pass on the information to the rescue centre.

I have done three more communications with Smurf and he is really enjoying his new life. The last time we spoke he was busy telling me about all the things he was doing: jumping over things; going through things; and making friends. It turned out he had joined the local agility class and was really good at it; every Thursday Jane said he would be at the door waiting to go in the car to his weekly class. His eating was good and he got on well with the cat.

Smurf had also learnt to fetch the post when it came through the letter box and was full of tricks. At last he had a settled home, and since being with Jane he had never chewed anything up.

Feedback

Below is some of the feedback that I have received from people who have had communications with me. All are genuine and email copies of each are kept. There are many more, these are just a selection of those that have been sent to me.

30 Jan 2011

I have to say that I was sceptical when I first researched this topic, but the things you have said couldn't have been found out any other way. I am so thrilled to have learned about Bess and her past, and it has made me that much more confident that I am caring for her in the right way. I would not hesitate to have another reading done. Regarding the shows, I have never been to shows myself, so I am planning to take her to my very first show once her foal is weaned and give her that pleasure after you revealed that she enjoys them. I'm sure she will guide me through them with ease, thanks.
Name withheld

28 Nov 2010

Was not really sure I believed you could speak to my horse, but you did and gave me things no one else could know, so thank you for that, and also to tell you that she is now feeling better and is again the horse I first bought. It is lovely to have her back, thank you thank you.
Susan

20 November 2010

I have had other horse communications with various people and was losing heart, but then I stumbled on Janine's page, I decided to try her. I am so glad that I did, not only did she help my horse and

myself but she proved to me that she had spoken to my horse. I got the wow factor. Brilliant, amazing.
Many thanks from Charlotte, West Midlands

19 Nov 2010

Thank you for the new update on my mare, and also the healing, it has worked, why should I be surprised. Also Ali my cat you did a reading for says hi.
Caroline Collins, Stafford

5 Sept 2010

Had a reading as a present for my birthday and I am so happy with it, a lovely gift and so much insight, thanks to you I can see my way forward now.
Regards, Rachael, Penrith

29 Aug 2010

Was amazed you could do an accurate reading for my horse, who was not even in your country. Thank you so much, it has helped me a lot, everything you said was so accurate.
W. Spain

11 Aug 2010

I would like to say a huge thank you to Janine, who got a lot of information about Cracker right, she knew things that would be impossible to guess and has given me lots of tips for improving the way that he goes – now let's see if they work.
Thanks, A. N.

2 August 2010

Dear Janine,
Thank you so much for your communication with Freddie. It was just so spot on about his personality, he is exactly like you said,

which I thought was amazing as you've never met him! And how you picked up on his feet and numnah was unbelievable!! Overall, it was really helpful, and the information you gave me from Jas my mare has also been of great help, I had never realized she was such a worrier. I will definitely be in touch with you again at a later date to check how they are getting on. Take care.
K. W. Carms.

July 2010

Hi Janine,
Thought you may like to know that Tromie seems much more relaxed and confident. He is often waiting to go out down the drive and sometimes goes first. He always used to be last and had to really think about it. Also his bum seems to have dropped to a more normal height, so hopefully this means his tum is feeling better. He certainly looks as if he is and seems to stand as if he is 6 inches taller. I can't really explain it any better but you probably know what I mean. He also has decided that bumping me with his head very softly is great fun! Anyway, thought you would like to know. Spots and Ted say hi too.
S. L., Wales

13 July 2010

If like me you have thought, 'If only I knew what my horse is thinking,' and didn't think there was a way of knowing, I have found a way with Janine. Billy my daughter's horse is a complicated, nervous and sometimes frightened horse but is also very kind and loving and we are having varying difficulties to cross with him. At the moment he is reluctant to be mounted. I had read about horse communicators in magazines and online and decided I would contact someone. I found Janine online and decided to contact her. When Janine only asked for a photo, age and how long he's been with us, I admit I had doubts! When the first part of our reading came I was blown away as to how much detail she knew of Billy, from seeing that in the past he was around a yard where lots of horses came and went; Billy was born on a breeding yard! Janine saw that he is stiff in his withers and not so good on his left rein. I could go on about more details Janine read but it will go on and on! Janine also told us that Billy understands what we say to him. I believe this as he was worried about changing homes and we had thought about selling him! But after Janine's help in understanding him HE ISN'T GOING ANYWHERE!! When we showed the others on our yard, they too were amazed on the accuracy of Billy's reading and are all thinking about contacting Janine themselves.

Thank you Janine, you have really helped us and Billy so much.

Teresa, Pembrokeshire

28 June 2010

Tia's feedback: I spent 3 years working on my mare, she had changed from being unrideable to going quite well but there were a few things that were holding us back and I couldn't put my finger on it. I contacted Janine in the hope that maybe she could provide some insight and help us put the last few things together. The communication I received back from Tia through Janine was so accurate and informative, Tia keeps her feed buckets and water drinker immaculately clean, it was one of the first things she told Janine – that she liked to eat and drink out of clean things! Our communication was worth every penny as I was also allowed to respond and ask more questions. We now have a bond and it has reached an incredible depth, we have moved up a height grade in our jumping and I have no doubt we will move again before the end of the year. I understand her and she knows she's safe with me and to have that communicated in a way she understands is priceless. Thank you. Janine's readings are full of information; as well as being able to ask the questions, she gives you an excellent insight into what's happening and what's going to happen. It's excellent as a general overview of things or if something is bothering you. Janine is so accurate I often turn to her for help on difficult matters.

Cheryl. xox

Janine Wilbraham

3 May 2010

Thank you so much for communicating with Sefton. It is amazing the insight you gained, and the accuracy of the information received. It has given me a great sense of calmness and contentment as I can truly understand the idiosyncrasies of Sefton's personality, and vice-versa! It has also taught me to trust my gut, and the experience gave me a real sense of joy and happiness. The next morning when I went over to the yard I fed the boys as usual. Sefton was clearly keen to get in with the other boys and once in with them, they played. Sefton and two of the others were running around, bucking and squealing. It was great as there was no sense of aggression displayed by Sefton, just pure happiness. I am sure this was his response to the message that he really is staying. Towards the end of their game, Sefton walked over to the fourth horse, who is an elderly gentleman not able to run around with the others. Sefton herded him over to where the others were by laying his head on Jo's back. I've never seen Sefton be so gentle and he seemed to be willing Jo to come and join the others. I just feel Sefton is starting to let go, which is wonderful to observe. Thank you so much for your intervention, Janine. You have an amazing gift and it has provided a breakthrough of understanding and confidence between Sefton and me.
Best wishes and I am sure I'll be in touch again.
Name withheld

2010

Janine got Ben's personality straight away, including him not liking to be caught by some people at the yard! It was interesting that she picked up on him not liking to be kept in a stable for long periods, while he is out daily for 8+ hours now, his previous life as a racehorse meant he was confined to his stable for long periods! I was amazed that Janine had picked up some pain with his fetlock, only two weeks before the reading he came in with it hot and swollen. Janine also picked up on his reluctance to move forward, although I still haven't got to the bottom of why. It was good to hear that he is happy with his new life and that he trusts me. Thanks Janine.

Name withheld

27 April 2010

Janine has been an amazing help, as I recently had to sell my horse (which was not his fault), and after a few months I was really worrying about him as we had been very close over the past eight years and I wasn't sure if he was happy and settled. Janine has told me that although he is happy in his new home, he misses me and the way I was with him . . . Along with some other very interesting things that I didn't know about him!! I'm now in the process of trying to buy him back; even with all his little quirks he is still the most amazing horse I have ever known. Wish me luck :) and thank you very much once again.
J. T. xxx

29 March 2010

Thank you so much for doing Samson's reading. I was amazed by what you told me but not at all surprised by a lot it. Your advice and suggestions are really helpful. It is so reassuring to know that Samson and I have such a good connection as that is something I have worked very hard on and it's great to know a little bit more about him as I'm sure it will be a great advantage to both of us. Since your communication with him, he's shown me quite a lot of affection which he's usually very economical with so I think he appreciated it too. I'd highly recommend you to anyone.
Helga (and Samson, of course)

11 November 2010

I've had Janine to do Reiki and communication with my pony Telyn, a beautiful black Section D mare, for a couple of years now, and each time she comes to see her she gets her money's worth! She never accepts less than an hour of Reiki and really enjoys it, telling Janine exactly where the healing is required and not letting her stop until it's done. As she is now 21 and has arthritis it has been beneficial for her as well.

I've asked many questions during these sessions as I bought Telyn when she was 16, so there was a lot of her life I had no idea about and wanted some answers to. Some questions concerned her behaviour and others were just general about her health and feelings.

She's told Janine stories about horses that have upset her, owners that she's been spiteful to and why, about her field-mate Rob who "twitters on" with big stories about what he's done, and that she likes going to shows because people "admire her and say she's pretty"!! She also likes going off in her horsebox as she "meets different horses" and likes that I "drive slowly".

She has also asked Janine if she could have seaweed and nettles to help her, which I provided her with. In answer to my question about why she was napping going out on her own she said I was "wishy washy"!! The main thing that has come through is that she is happy with me, happy with her life and where she is. I would recommend any horse owner getting Janine for the general feel-good factor of the Reiki if nothing else.

A. Jones

www.horsecommunicator-reikihealer.co.uk

Lightning Source UK Ltd.
Milton Keynes UK
UKOW020024131011

180158UK00001BB/12/P